PRAISE FOR PERFECT AND FORGIVEN

"Zach Maldonado has been radically and authentically undone by grace. He is also gifted to communicate like few others. Those realities combined allow truth, lived out, to jump from the page. He is smart, vulnerable, and funny, funny, and funny. But he is intensely and thoughtfully creative in finding pictures and language that get this message of a life-giving freedom to all of us. If Zach was in your life, you'd be a better person. I trust what he writes. Because he is trying it out, in every area of his life. I think you will love this book."

—**John Lynch**, Author of "On My Worst Day" and co-author of "The Cure"

"'Perfect and Forgiven' isn't just a book; it's an invitation to live the life of freedom and purpose God has designed for you. Zach unpacks powerful Biblical truths, raw and transparent stories from his own testimony and many inspirational examples to help you unlock the God-given potential lying dormant inside. You could read this entire book in a few hours, but it has the potential to change your life forever!"

—**Dave Willis**, Best-selling author of "The Seven Laws of Love" and TV and Podcast Host for MarriageToday.

"'Perfect and Forgiven' is a wonder of practical beauty and theological truth! I laughed, gasped, marveled and cried when reading Zach Maldonado's book, because the God I know, who speaks to me and motivates me, moved through its' pages. If you know—or have yet to know—the God of all grace, get this book. You'll be deeply moved."

—**Ralph Harris**, Best-selling author of Life According to Perfect, and God's Astounding Opinion of You

"This book is such a beautiful reminder of God's relentless, radical grace. It inspires and challenges us to reject the narrative of shame, accept that we are accepted, and live out our identity as sons and daughters of God."

—**Dominic Done**, Lead Pastor at Westside:
A Jesus Church and author of When Faith Fails

"Through Zach's delightful gift of storytelling you will enjoy a crystal-clear understanding of what Jesus did for you, giving you permission to finally enjoy life."

—**Brandon Ball**, Lead Pastor at
ChurchUnlimited

"I am so glad that Zach has written this book to show who Jesus transforms us into at the moment of salvation. If you want to learn your true identity and how-to live-in freedom and victory, then you've got to read this book!"

—**Jason White**, Lead Pastor at Manchaca
Baptist Church

"When someone comes into a revelation of grace there are often a couple of steps that happen. First is the sheer euphoria at the discovery, followed then by the bitter anger and disillusioned bewilderment that they were not told this before. Thankfully Zach Maldonado seems to have skipped that second part altogether. The love and fire he carries seems to continue to burn brighter and hotter with every writing. An outstanding follow up to "The Cross Worked.", this book may be a perfect companion, answering many of the questions that his previous work may have raised. But my favorite element of "Perfect and Forgiven" is the honest and personal vulnerability. There are three pieces of advice that I have carried in ministry when it comes to releasing revelation. 1. Preach the Word. 2. Make it personal. 3. Give people a quest. Zach covers all three here with accuracy, passion, and joy. I'm thrilled to endorse this important book."

—**Bill Vanderbush**, Pastor at Community Presbyterian Church

"If someone asks you to describe how God views you and you find yourself searching for the right words, this book will remove any question you have about what God thinks of you! Zach Maldonado is incredibly skillful at taking huge, biblical concepts and communicating them in meaningful, powerfully connecting, understandable ways!"

—**Bill Pruitt**, Lead Pastor at Graceworks Church

"So many Christians struggle with the reality of who they are in Christ, and the result is shaken confidence in their relationship with God. In *Perfect and Forgiven*, Zach Maldonado beautifully navigates through topics that will help any Christian either be more firmly established in their identity in Christ, or answer questions about doubts they may have about how God sees them."

—**Matt Graves**, Lead Pastor at Heritage Church

"Jesus said, "You will know the truth and the truth will set you free" (John 8:32). Paul wrote, "You are transformed by the renewing of your mind" (Romans 12:2). The nature of truth, real truth, when received with an open heart is both freeing and transforming. In *Perfect and Forgiven*, Zach takes misunderstood and often overlooked biblical truth, and makes it accessible at a heart level. Read this book, not simply with an open mind, but an open heart, and you will never be the same."

—**Joel Lowry**, Lead Pastor at Sozo Church

"Zach teaches us all what I wish I knew when I was a teenage believer: We can live FROM forgiveness rather than FOR forgiveness. This takes the message of grace even further and makes us all freer."

—**Matt Wade**, Lead Pastor at The Table Church

"Zach's latest book will help you to embrace the truth, so you can walk in your freedom and experience your inheritance. You will be refreshed, inspired and challenged to try less but trust more in the Good News of Jesus."

—**Lon Williams**, Lead Pastor at Liberty Church

"Ironically, the popular message of Christianity has placed so many people into bondage. Although we believe our tickets are punched for heaven, we are constantly enslaved by our own fear that nothing has changed about who we are. "Perfect and Forgiven" is the exact book to break those chains of bondage. There is freedom found on every page. What a refreshing gift this book is!"

—**Caleb Lynch**, Lead Pastor at Open Door Fellowship Church

"I believe with all my heart that the believer's Identity in Christ is one of the most important concepts in all of Christianity. In this book, Zach Maldonado does a masterful job teaching us how to discover and appropriate our spiritual identity. From cover to cover, this book is packed with life changing truth. Read it, study it, and BELIEVE it!"

—**Cory Hallett**, Lead Pastor at On Mission Church

"I am convinced that Zach Maldonado is a fresh and current voice to the next generation with the message of life in Christ. His life stories are both profound and humorous and his passion for Jesus shines through. Like many, Zach has experienced the pain and burden of a religion that demands further sacrifices beyond the cross of Jesus and he has found freedom that has produced a joyful and vibrant life. His words will bring more than relief, they will produce life that reflects the heart of Jesus: "My yoke is easy and my burden is light." This will be a book that you will want to read again and again as the truths are profound and life changing."

—**Jimmy Pruitt**, Lead Pastor at Bridge Church Fredericksburg

"I cannot think of a more needed message for broken and weary people everywhere. Zach Maldonado steps on my toes and chips away at the longtime yet false myths of performance driven Christianity. If you come from the belief that God is keeping track of your sin, this book is for you. It's a reminder that grace isn't a means to the end; it's the end."

—**Darryl Bellar**, Lead Pastor at The Journey Church

"Wouldn't it be great if every believer knew the marvelous reality of who they were in Christ? In Perfect and Forgiven, Zach Maldonado has done a wonderful job of exposing the lies that often prevent us from fully experiencing the Life that we have in Jesus. Through gripping personal illustrations, he pulls us back into the heart of The Father for His children and reminds us of who we truly are. Grab your Bible, a good cup of coffee, and this book and get ready to hear the truth of your identity clearly spoken over you by a great young brother in Christ."

—**Anthony Pratt**, Lead Pastor, Riverview Community Church

Discovering Your Freedom
From Shame, Guilt, and Sin

~~Not~~
PERFECT

~~Just~~
and

FORGIVEN

ZACH MALDONADO

PERFECT AND FORGIVEN

© 2019 by Zach Maldonado

To my beautiful Grace.

Thank you for always loving me and

reminding me of who I am in Christ.

Contents

Foreword

There's nothing more empty and lifeless than rule-based religion—and nothing more fulfilling than knowing Jesus as life and letting Him rule. Yet so many believers today feel empty as they perpetually chase after more forgiveness, more righteousness, and more favor with God. This book by my friend Zach Maldonado can change all of that.

Instead of begging for what you already have in Christ, you'll discover within these pages that you're complete in Him. This means no more searching or pleading to be more qualified or more equipped.

Instead of fearing you'll be condemned, you'll start reveling in your freedom from punishment. Yes, the wages of sin is death, but Jesus died and paid those wages in full. Since no wages remain, you'll never be punished, ever.

Instead of worrying about losing out on God, you'll be awed by His refusal to abandon you for any reason. Even when you're faithless, He remains faithful, and nothing can ever separate you from His love.

Instead of trying to get God to like you, you'll enjoy His warm embrace like never before. Here, you'll learn that you're no longer dirty and distant from God, but clean and close. You'll realize that just beneath your skin and bones and everything that you've called "you", that's where Christ lives. You can't get any closer than being one with Jesus!

And if God's Spirit actually gave birth to you, then what kind of person are you? Might your righteousness be real even here and now? After all, doesn't God see you for who you really are? And doesn't He like what He sees?

This book shouts a resounding "yes." You're re-born from above with new passions and desires. You're a handcrafted work designed by the Master Painter Himself. He dances over you and delights in you. He relishes the opportunity to display the brushstrokes of His life on your unique canvas.

We all need to know these precious truths – every day, every hour, every moment. The trustworthy voice of Zach Maldonado helps us get there. His book is easy to read, shines a bright light on Jesus, and offers the Scriptural answers you've been searching for.

—**Andrew Farley,** bestselling author of *The Naked Gospel and Twisted Scripture,* lead pastor of Church Without Religion and radio host of *Andrew Farley LIVE*

AndrewFarley.org

What's Wrong with Me?

I've been hurt deeply. I've experienced the shame of sin. I've made stupid mistakes. I've been cheated on and lied to, and I've always struggled with lies about who I am. Can you relate? Maybe it's depression, sexual sin, or addictions; all of these struggles—and many more—convince us that something is wrong with us.

Everything I'd gone through was evidence enough to convince me that there was something uniquely wrong with who I was. Not only did I think other people felt this way, but I believed God did too. Shame convinced me of the lie that there was nothing I or anyone else could do to make me loveable, accepted, or whole.

At one point in my life, I thought the answer to my problem was trying harder. You know, going to church, praying, and believing harder. Then I determined that I needed to do more for God, so I volunteered more and witnessed more and went to church twice a week. Then I thought that maybe I needed to be better, so I tried my hardest to not sin and to live perfectly.

After years of trying harder, doing more, and being better, I gave up. It's not that going to church, praying, volunteering, witnessing, and doing things for God are wrong. They're not. But when you don't understand the true message of Christianity, all that is just religion. And religion offers no life. What we need is not more rules and things to do, but Jesus Christ. We need good news, not good advice. We need life, not behavior modification. We need relationship, not religion.

I, like so many others, boiled the message of Christianity down to one slogan: "not perfect, just forgiven." Most of the time, I barely believed I was forgiven. But I knew for sure I was far from perfect and that God saw me as a filthy, worthless sinner.

Then one day I realized that the good news of Jesus Christ is more than being forgiven and then going to heaven when I die. The message isn't just about what Christ did for us, but also what He did *to* us through the cross and resurrection.

Our search for identity is what drives everything we do. Athletes want to become better, so they work hard and do everything they can to become something they aren't. The same is true of the businessman, the entrepreneur, and the human in general. We're all trying to become something. We're all trying to prove ourselves and make ourselves better. As a result, most of us base our identity on something that's always changing— our status, recent accomplishment or failure, or behavior.

The false identity we carry is also the reason for our pain, shame, and struggles. I always thought my past, my sin, and my shame was who I was. I believed I was impure, unlovable, and never good enough. My experience in ministry has shown me that many people feel the same way.

But what if we could live our lives from a foundation that will never change? What if there's nothing uniquely wrong with who you are? And what if what Christ did to you is real

3

and can change how you see yourself and live each day?

This book offers a new way to live. A new way to see yourself. Healing for your hurts and a path toward freedom from your past, your self-hate, and the pressure of measuring up. The truth of who I am in Christ set me free from all my mistakes, hurts, and struggles, and it's still setting me free today. That's why I wrote this book—to help you also discover what God truly thinks of you, know the truth that sets you free, and overcome false beliefs about who you are.

Nothing

There is nothing at all wrong with you.

Song of Solomon 4:7 NCV

"'Nana, 'nana, 'nana!"

I was about to die. I wasn't feeling right and couldn't act right. My vision was blurry, and my body felt like I'd been hit by a Mack truck. Something was terribly wrong, but I didn't know what. All I could do was curl up in fetal position and say, "'Nana, 'nana, 'nana"—banana, if you don't know kid talk.

Once I got the 'nana, I knew I'd be better.

But that got thrown up too.

What was my four-year-old self thinking? Did he realize what people would say at his funeral? And did he really just choose a banana as his last meal? But I guess in his defense, if a 'nana couldn't help, what could?

As I moaned and groaned, my mom whispered, "Zach, it's just a stomach virus. There's nothing wrong with you."

"But, Mom, I'm sick."With how I felt, I couldn't believe nothing was wrong.

"Honey, it's not your fault," she tried to assure me. "You're sick because of a virus. You're okay."

This didn't make sense to me. How could I feel so awful and yet having nothing wrong with me? The reason: *I* was not the sickness. The sickness was in me, but it wasn't *me*. I was sick because of a virus, not because there was fault in who I was.

Many years later, I learned that the same is true for Christians. What if there's nothing actually wrong with you and me? What if we sin because of something that's not *us*?

I'm still learning what my mom taught me that day. You see, sin is like a stomach virus. It's in us, but it's not us. It can tempt us to act in weird ways and make us feel bad and wrong, but sin is not us and we are not sin. We may think we need to fix ourselves, but God is asking us to just fix our focus on Him. We may think we're the problem, but sin is. We may think something's wrong with who we are, but we've been lied to.

The church has believed the lie that *we* are the problem, that we're dirty, bad, sinful people who are just "saved by grace." We've believed this cheap message that Christianity is only about what happens when we die. But what if the message of Jesus changes everything about how we live and see ourselves every day?

I didn't have any choice in choosing how the stomach bug affected me. But in our Christian life, we do have a choice. Sin has no power over us, and in any moment we can choose to trust Jesus or we can sin. We may feel like we're bad or that something's wrong with us, but our feelings are not indicators of truth. God's

"
He says there's nothing at all wrong with us.
"

Word is. And He says there's nothing at all wrong with us.

When Adam and Eve sinned for the first time, was it their identity that caused them to sin? No, it was the power of sin and the tempter that led them to sin. There was nothing wrong with Adam, yet he sinned. That's why our struggle is not with ourselves, but with sin.

Not only that, but Adam and Eve believed a lie. They were both perfect and righteous like God, but they believed the lie from the Enemy that they weren't like God and that sin would make them like God. That's one of the Enemy's greatest tricks—to try to make us think we need something when we already have it.

In Christ, God makes us new, flawless people. Yet we still sin. We've believed the lie that we ourselves are the reason. But we aren't; sin is. Sure, we make a choice and play a role in sinning. But we are good and holy, and nothing is wrong with who we are spiritually. We're perfect people who still sin. That's the good news of Jesus: He doesn't define us by our behavior; instead, we're defined by who we are in Him.

There's no flaw or mistake about who you are. Who you are in Christ is not affected by what you do or don't do. Your identity is irreversible and unshakeable, because it was given to you by God's grace; it was never your doing.

Think about it. We did nothing to become sinners. The

Bible says we're born that way; we're born in sin. In the same way, we did nothing to become flawless believers. We were *reborn* that way. We're reborn in Christ. The Bible calls this being born again.

Put simply, we get our identity from what we're *in*. The moment we believe in Jesus, we become new creations. Our identity is not progressively becoming good or flawless. In Christ, we're good, blameless, right, perfect people the moment we believe in Him.

Your struggle is with sin, not with the new person God has made you. There's no flaw in you. If you're in Christ and Christ is in you, then everything true of Christ is now true of you. Popular teaching says that when God

> "
> *If you're in Christ and Christ is in you, then everything true of Christ is now true of you.*
> "

looks at you, He sees Jesus. Or He has to look at us through Jesus. But this isn't true; God sees all of you and loves what He sees, because He created you new and perfect.

Pride, anger, lust—these are all things you may struggle with, but they are not you. You're the perfect child of God who struggles with those things. See the difference?

Learning my identity took me many years of searching. Drugs, alcohol, girls, shame, guilt, and religion all led me to learn the simple truth that nothing at all was wrong with me. Nothing.

Many of us have heard about our identity in Christ, but then we move on to "deeper" things. But identity is the core message. It's the good news we need to hear every day, because we live in a world that's telling us the opposite.

I was taught my identity by mistakes, problems, and messiness—not by success, goodness, or religion. God uses everything to show us who we already are in Him. That's why the Christian life is not about working hard to become someone or something else; it's about living from all that God has *already* made you to be. We're not told to fight to get free or to get our sins forgiven or to be made new in Christ. The fight is to trust those things are already true. The best news is, God is relentlessly fighting for you to believe the truth that you're free, forgiven, and new.

" God is relentlessly fighting for you to believe the truth that you're free, forgiven, and new. "

Who are you? Our initial response to this question is typically based on our job, our addiction, or our status in society. "I'm an athlete ... I'm just an angry person ... I'm an alcoholic ... I'm a sinner ... I'm a minister ... I'm divorced ... I'm a teacher ... I'm rich ... I'm poor ... I'm a mother"—you get the idea. We base our identity around what we do or what we've done. Not only that, but we live out of who we think and believe we are. If you think you're bad, you'll live bad. If you think you're a sinner, you'll live like one.

But God is inviting us to base our beliefs on what He has done for us and to us. He's asking us to rethink how we see ourselves in light of how He sees us. The world may reject you, but you are accepted. The world may say you're not good enough, but you are enough. The world may say you're a criminal, but you're a child of God.

When you begin to understand who you are and *Whose* you are, you begin to live out of that new reality. Your old habits and behaviors start to change, and your actions start to reflect whom God has already made you.

I'm not saying behavior doesn't matter. It does. But

our behavior is the fruit of what we believe. We need to first believe who we are in Christ, then our behavior will follow. Put another way, our identity determines our behavior, but our behavior never determines or defines our identity.

The world, the Enemy, and sin feed us lies about who we are. If what we hear doesn't liberate us, then it's not from God. Jesus wants us to be free. And it's through knowing the truth about Him and who we are that we'll begin living in the freedom He won for us.

This isn't a book on how you can do ten things to help yourself. If you're in Christ, this is a book about what God has already done to you and for you. It's about Christ and how His death and resurrection made you perfect forever, and about how understanding this can liberate you, encourage you, and teach you to live in the freedom of who you are.

Hearing God's Opinion

"My child, no matter what you or others think, there's nothing wrong with you. In every mistake or sin or problem you face, My opinion of you never wavers. No matter what you do or what you've done, I'll always be in you, I'll always be for you, and I'll always love you. Say goodbye to all those lies religion taught you, and say hello to the truth of your new identity in Me."

2

Complete

And in Him you have been made complete,
and He is the head over all rule and authority.

Colossians 2:10

I was running late for high school football practice, and was missing the most important thing in my life—my cell phone. If you know me, I have a slight addiction to my phone. (I'm working on it; don't judge me.)

My investigation ranged all over the house—in every pair of jeans, under every piece of furniture, in every crack and place it could be. Nothing. I went to ask my mom, because moms have this special power of knowing where everything is, but even she didn't know where my phone was. I felt hopeless.

I ran to my twin sister, thinking she was trying to dig up some dirt on me. Surprisingly, she wasn't. She hadn't seen it either.

I bolted to my one-year-old brother. "Christian, have you seen my cell phone?"

"Bubba," he responded. Not quite the answer I wanted, but cute nonetheless.

Right as I was about to go crazy, a familiar vibration came from the depths of my pocket. I reached down and felt it—my cell phone.

Now you may think I'm an idiot, and that wouldn't be too far off. But it's sad to me that many Christians spend their entire lives searching everywhere for something they already have in Christ.

This was me. I was saved at the age of twelve, but I spent six years searching for what I already had. I tried it all and nothing satisfied. I did everything I could to be more successful, more popular, and more of whatever the world said I needed to be. All this because I believed the lie that I needed more—that I wasn't good enough, significant enough, or valuable enough.

While I believed God loved me, I was told I needed to do more in order for Him to keep loving me and stay pleased with me. I tried my best. But I always felt that His back was toward me and that He was ready to send a lightning bolt my way. Like most of us, I thought that although we're saved by grace, our relationship with God is based on our performance. Eventually, believing He loved me only for what I did for Him, I decided I wanted nothing to do with Him.

Desperately wanting approval, I chased after girls and accolades. I wanted popularity, so I partied with the cool kids. I wanted relief from stress, so I tried drugs. I wanted attention, so I did my best to excel at sports. Nothing worked. Nothing satisfied. Nothing the world offered me was ever enough. Every night I felt the same—lonely, empty, and worn out. I could never do or be enough to feel complete. I determined that something was uniquely wrong with me. I saw everyone else's happiness and wondered why I was the only exception.

On my eighteenth birthday, my search started coming to an end. A friend threw me a party, and tons of people came—for me. Yet I felt alone, empty, and unsatisfied. In the middle of the night, I sensed God tugging at my heart to give Him one more chance. So I did.

And I discovered the God of the Bible. The One who loves me without condition. The One who's *for* me. The One who's pleased with me apart from what I do. The One who knows me and likes me despite my shortcomings. The One who saved me and rescued me so that He could be in relationship with me. He called me out of my shame. And now He tells me (and you), "You're no longer what your shame says you are."

When I realized the goodness of Jesus, everything changed. He isn't asking me to earn or work for His acceptance, presence, or love; instead, He's asking me to enjoy it. He's in me every moment, and because of that, I'm complete. I no longer need to search for meaning, value, or anything else I may need. Since I have all of Jesus in every moment, I have all I need.

> "
> *He isn't asking me to earn or work for His acceptance, presence, or love; instead, He's asking me to enjoy it.*
> "

When I believed God was angry at me, it was easy to sin and rebel. But when I realized how good and kind God really is toward me, I no longer wanted to sin against Him.

God is the one who bears our burdens. The shame and hurt from our past was never ours to carry. God will never get tired of bearing your burdens and sustaining you. He never said, "I'll save you and get you started, but then you'll need to take it from there." No, God promises that He will sustain you for all of eternity.

Do you realize how good, kind, and loving God is to you?

***

There was a man who lived on a farm, which was everything he owned. He was struggling to make enough money from the land to support himself. Despite his hard work, he was hungry, poor, and in danger of losing the farm.

Day after day this man didn't know what to do. He wondered how he would pay his bills and how he could earn more money. One day, an oil company came by and asked to dig for oil. The oil company believed there was a chance that oil could be tapped on the land. Sure enough, they discovered one of the biggest oil reserves ever found. Just like that, this poor farmer became one of the richest men in the world.

When this man first bought his property, he possessed all the oil rights. He owned that vast quantity of oil beneath his land—yet he didn't know it, and He lived in poverty. This is how I lived for years, and sadly this is how many people in the church live. We have abundance within us, and His name is Jesus. Yet we live as if we have nothing.

In Christ, we have everything we need to live fulfilled lives. We're complete. We lack nothing. And it's from our place of abundance in Christ that we're called to

> In Christ, we have everything we need to live fulfilled lives. We're complete. We lack nothing.

live. For too long we've believed the lie of religion. Religion declares, "You're broken," but God declares, "You're complete in Me." Not once in the New Testament is a believer described as broken. And not once does it say that God is "breaking" us. Instead we see that God is building us up and reminding us that we're complete in Him.

This means we don't need "more." We don't need more

of Jesus; we're already united with Him and sealed by His Spirit. We don't need more faith; God has already given us each a measure of faith as a gift. We don't need more of whatever religion or this world says we need.

Jesus is enough. He's all we need. And He's inviting us to wake up each day and know that we don't need to search any more. Instead, we need to understand that everything we've been searching for, we already have in Jesus.

God is inviting us to realize that the cell phone is in our pocket. The search is over. Take a seat and enjoy your Father in heaven.

I no longer feel the need to do the things I once did. My life has been radically changed by knowing that God loves me and is for me, and that I'm complete in Him. Of course, I still struggle and find myself searching again and again. But God's not frustrated with us for searching, because He uses our search to show us time and again that He is sufficient.

Yes, we're still learning and growing. Jesus was perfectly God, perfect in everything, yet we read that He grew in wisdom and that He learned obedience. We're complete and perfect, yet we're learning about who God has made us to be, and we're learning how to live from our new identity and not from our old habits. In the same way that an oak sapling doesn't get "oakier" as it grows up, you and I do not get holier, more accepted, or more complete as we mature; instead, we just learn to be who we are. We grow up.

A flower doesn't have to struggle and strive to grow upward from the ground; it naturally grows toward the sun. That's how the Bible says we grow—through Jesus, not self-effort. When we behold all that Jesus is, we learn to believe Him with everything. Our growth comes from God. There's no rush. Our growth is His job, and He's in control of the timing. So we can simply relax about our growth and trust Him with it.

> "
> We can simply relax about our growth and trust Him with it.
> "

We're called to fixate on Jesus, not on our sin or on what we need to do. And when we look to Jesus, we see that through Him we're complete and in need of nothing. Being complete in Christ changes everything for you and me. Instead of trying to get our acceptance, love, and value from other people, we get it from Christ. We no longer need other people to do something only God can do.

For married people, this means not expecting their spouse to be the source of their meaning and value; instead, they find it in Christ. For all of us who have friends, it means we don't rely on those friends to make us feel good about ourselves all the time; instead, we lean on Jesus and let His truth permeate our thoughts and feelings. For those of us who participate in sports or some other form of competition, instead of seeking worth from the cheers of the crowd, we can rest in the value of God's celebration of us.

All of us can look to, rely on, and have all our needs met in Christ alone.

Hearing God's Opinion

"You're My absolute favorite! Take a look at yourself. You're complete. You're new. You don't need to do anything else to become more. You're enough. You can stop the search and trust Me. I've given you everything you need, and there's nothing left for you to do, except to live from all that I've made you to be. The world will say you need more—but never forget, you have Me, therefore you're complete."

3

Pleasing

For we are to God the pleasing aroma of Christ
among those who are being saved and those who are perishing.

2 Corinthians 2:15 NIV

Did you know that before Jesus started His earthly ministry, before He did a single miracle, God declared to the world that Jesus was His beloved Son in whom He was pleased? God was pleased with Jesus long before He fed the five thousand, healed a leper, or rose from the dead. God was pleased with Jesus because Jesus was His Son, not because of what Jesus did.

The same is true of you. God is pleased with you because of who you are—His

> "
> God is pleased with you
> because of who you
> are—His beloved child.
> "

beloved child. We live our lives out of God's unconditional affection for us. The moment you placed faith in Jesus, He was pleased with you. Put another way, you make God happy. That's why you don't have to impress God. He's in awe of you already.

Most of my life was spent trying to keep God pleased. My struggle was that I never thought He was pleased. I tried so hard to do more and be more for God that eventually I gave up on Him. I didn't want anything to do with a God who needed me to behave perfectly in order for Him to love me. But one day I discovered that God was pleased with me because of what Jesus had done for me and to me.

This didn't cause me to want to take advantage of all that Jesus did for me. Instead, I fell in love with Jesus. And as you know, when you love someone, you don't do less for them; you do more.

This is how God intended things. He wanted us to be motivated by love, not fear. It's His perfect love that takes away our fear. Most of us have believed that we need to be scared of God. But the biblical concept of fearing God is not about being afraid; it's about being in awe of how good and loving God is. The Christian life isn't about us trying to keep an angry God pleased; it's about us trusting in a loving God who's already pleased.

> "
> *The Christian life isn't about us trying to keep an angry God pleased; it's about us trusting in a loving God who's already pleased.*
> "

I know what you've been told: "God loves you, but here are ten things you need to do to keep Him on your side." That isn't true. We don't get saved by God's goodness and then keep Him happy by our effort and performance. The Bible says that without trust, it's impossible to please God. Put another way, our trust is the only thing that pleases God. Not our effort or best performance. God is looking for us to trust Him, not strive for Him.

God is asking us to change our focus from doing things for Him to simply trusting and enjoying Him. Here's the crazy thing: When we trust Him, He leads us to all that He wants us to do, which pleases Him. The best news is, He has given you all the faith you need to trust Him. He has made you faithful and trustworthy. It's your identity to trust God. It's what you crave.

I know this can be tough to learn. I struggle with people pleasing. Many of us don't even realize we've been trained to work hard to please everyone. It's how the world is. We work hard to get good grades and impress our teachers. We work hard and play hard to impress our parents and coaches. No matter what it is, we're all working hard to impress and please others.

But God's system is different. We're not working toward something; we're working from it. We're living and working and playing from God's approval of and pleasure with us. It's like playing a game knowing we already won and that we're the MVP.

That's why Jesus is all about relationship, not religion. He wants us to simply know Him and live from His love. That's the paradox of pleasing God: we're already pleasing to Him, and we can still please Him.

We don't work from obligation or duty. We work because of God's love for us. When I work for someone I love,

I don't consider it work; I think of it as love. I want to do it. I desire to do it. It gives me energy to love those who love me. That's the difference between Jesus and religion. We work from delight, not duty.

In *Gladiator,* one of my favorite movies, General Maximus becomes a slave and then a gladiator after being betrayed. On one occasion in the arena, after working swiftly and skillfully to kill his opponents, Maximus throws his sword into the stands and calls out, "Are you not entertained?"

Many of us feel this way toward God. We may ask Him, "Are you not happy? Are you not pleased by all I'm doing for you?" Sometimes it can feel like we never do enough. But the good news is, He's entertained. Not by what you do, but by *you.* He loves every second He gets to live in you. God smiles when He thinks of you. And since you're always on His mind, His smile is always in your direction.

> "
> God smiles when He thinks of you. And since you're always on His mind, His smile is always in your direction.
> "

Hearing God's Opinion

"You no longer need to wonder what I think of you. I'm so pleased with you. You make Me so happy! You don't need to impress Me; I'm already impressed! Nothing I've created compares to you. I promise you this: that even in your worst moment, My pleasure in you will not change. You make Me smile, kid. I love you so much!"

Accepted

Accept one another, then, just as Christ accepted you.

Romans 15:7 NIV

Growing up, I had a lazy eye. I think I still have it, but it's not as lazy anymore. Anyway, part of the therapy for my lazy eye was wearing an eye patch. You know, like pirates wear.

In the third grade, I started wearing this thing for an hour or two each day during class time—and wow, you would have thought I was an actual pirate by the way my classmates looked at me. I could feel their judgment and rejection. Later, the jokes started coming in. I'd previously been called names for wearing glasses—but now this? It was devastating.

I remember sitting outside one day, watching the other kids play, when my best friend, Michael, came up and asked me what was wrong. He was in another class and didn't know about my eye patch. I was scared to tell him about it, fearing that he would reject me too.

Finally, I fessed up and told him about having to wear the eye patch and what people were saying. I looked at him expecting rejection, but what I got was excitement and jealousy. Michael said, "Dude, you're like a pirate. And who doesn't want to be a pirate!"

Shocked and a little puzzled, I didn't know how to receive this acceptance at first. But from that day forward, I wore that patch proudly.

It's amazing what acceptance does to a person. In this world, most of us are familiar with rejection, which is why *acceptance* is a hard word for many of us. If you're like me, your experience is more rejection than acceptance.

Whether it's your physical appearance, something you've done recently, or something you haven't done, we all fear rejection and we all need acceptance. The good news of

Christianity is that on day one—moment one—we're as accepted as we'll ever be. God approves of us. And He promises to never reject us, no matter what.

> "
> *The good news of Christianity is that on day one—moment one—we're as accepted as we'll ever be.*
> "

He's saying, "In every moment, even in every mistake, my opinion of you never wavers. I'll always accept you and love you." Even at your worst, God still adores you. He still approves of who you are. He still wants you, no matter what.

Knowing our acceptance and our identity in Christ means that it's okay for us not to feel okay. Our new identity allows us to look at the lies our feelings are expressing and replace them with the truth of what God says.

I lived my entire life trying to prove myself. Prove myself to my parents, my friends, and to God. I never thought I was good enough. I always thought I had to do more. What the world offered was never enough. I had my high moments, but those things never satisfied.

The one thing that satisfies me now is being known, accepted, and loved by Jesus.

Tom Brady is a professional football player. He has everything the world says a man needs—money, a model for a wife, and all the attention he needs. He's considered by some to be the greatest of all time at what he does. In an interview after his third championship, he said he felt like there had to be more. He didn't feel that what he'd done or earned was enough. He didn't feel satisfied.[1]

Wait, I thought all those things would satisfy. They don't. They didn't for Tom, they didn't for me, and they won't for you or anyone else. That's why we continually see celebrities taking their life, getting busted for drugs, or admitting they're miserable.

Followers, likes, friends, popularity—what this world has to offer cannot satisfy our deepest need and desire. We all need and desire love and acceptance. The good news is that in Christ, we have all the love and value and acceptance we'll ever need.

You don't have to prove yourself to God. You're accepted, pleasing, and made right by faith; there's nothing

"
You're accepted, pleasing, and made right by faith; there's nothing to prove.
"

1   Super Bowl 2019: 60 Minutes Looks Back at Tom Brady in 2005," 60 Minutes, January 30, 2019, https://www.cbsnews.com/news/super-bowl-2019-looking-back-at-tom-brady-in-2005-60-minutes/

to prove. This means God likes you for you, not what you can do for Him or what you bring to the table. Hard to believe, huh? But that's the beauty of God's grace. It's scandalous. It doesn't make sense. We live from God's unconditional acceptance of us, not for it. This means we obey, serve, give, and love others from God's approval and acceptance of us, not for it.

Our biggest fear is that if we're "found out," people will reject us. They'll think we're frauds. We desperately want to be known, but we also fear that if we're fully known, no one will like us. So we hide. We fake it.

But God fully knows you. Every mistake. Every weird thing. He knows it all, and yet He still loves you. He even likes you. You're His favorite. You're fully known and fully loved by Him.

Do you realize what this means? You're free to fail. You're free to mess up. You don't have to get it right in order for God to accept you or love you. That's what's so radical about the gospel: it's not about you! You don't have to perform perfectly in order to be loved, accepted, or pleasing to God.

> " You don't have to perform perfectly in order to be loved, accepted, or pleasing to God. "

The pressure's off. And when we recognize that the pressure's off, we start realizing, *I no longer want to fail, because I know I'm accepted and loved by the God of the universe.*

God is reminding us that what others may see as flaws, He sees as cool. So don't be afraid of your eye patch.

God's next to you, wearing one too.

Hearing God's Opinion

"You're safe to be you. I don't want you to hide. I don't want you to be like someone else. I accept you. All of you. I love living inside of you. You and I make such a great team. I'm so proud to be your God. I'm never ashamed to be associated with you. Your sin doesn't surprise Me. I've seen it all and I've taken it all away. I know everything about you, and guess what? None of it makes Me change My mind about you. I enjoy you!"

5

Loved

For I am convinced that neither death nor life, neither angels nor demons, neither the present nor the future, nor any powers, neither height nor depth, nor anything else in all creation, will be able to separate us from the love of God that is in Christ Jesus our Lord.

Romans 8:38–39 NIV

"Marry a prostitute."

Sorry, Lord, I misunderstood you. What did you say?

"Hosea, I want you to marry a prostitute and have a family." This is what God tells Hosea—a teacher of God, a man of respect. God doesn't give him an explanation, He just tells him to do this. So Hosea marries Gomer. (Bummer of a name, huh?)

As the story progresses, they have kids and things seem normal. Then one day Hosea wakes up to find Gomer gone. She'd left him and gone back into prostitution.

So God tells Hosea, "Go again. Go find Gomer and love her, just like My love for My people."

Hosea goes door to door, searching for his wife. He's searching in back alleys, in parts of town where he's never been. And he's talking to men and women who've seen better days. Then (as the story implies) he stumbles on an auction where Gomer is being sold to the highest bidder.

Hosea buys her. He buys back his wife, the person who'd left him, embarrassed him, and cheated on him. He doesn't care about the price or the past. Hosea doesn't demand anything from Gomer; he just buys her back. Unlike the other men before him, he doesn't purchase Gomer to employ her, but to cure her.

Then Hosea makes a promise to Gomer. He promises to never leave her and to always be faithful to her. He doesn't condemn her, but comforts her. He doesn't accuse her, but assures her.

This story is a picture of God and us. Hosea is an image of God, and Gomer represents us. While we were dirty rotten sinners, God pursued us, bought us, made us new, and made a promise to us that cannot be revoked. God found us in our chains and set us free. He entered our mess and made us clean. God didn't save us because we were good or had our life in order. God saved us because He loved us and wanted us.

God's love isn't changed by the things we do or don't do. He proved this by going to the cross when we were His enemies. He took our sin

> "
> *God's love isn't changed by the things we do or don't do.*
> "

long before you or I ever knew about Him. He loved you before you existed. When He was on the cross, you were on His mind.

No one is too far gone. And you haven't fallen too far to be disqualified from God's love. His love has no limits. Even the worst of people are loved and pursued by God.

That's the beauty of Jesus. He doesn't demand that we have our life in order for us to come to him. Religion says, "Clean yourself up, then go to God." Jesus says, "Come to Me, and I'll make you clean." Religion says, "Climb up to God and save yourself." Jesus says, "I climbed up that cross to save you."

God loves you because it's who God is. He cannot cease loving you, or He would stop being God. His love for you isn't based on your qualifications, status, or what you have to offer. His love for you is without condition. If you think you have to earn God's love, you'll spend your entire life performing for Him and never enjoying Him.

God doesn't need you. He wants you. He doesn't love you so that you can do things for Him. He loves you because He is captivated by you. It's His passion and joy to love you. It's all He wants to do. His heart beats for you.

There's never a moment when God won't love you. You cannot exhaust His love. He doesn't get tired of loving you. Jesus says He loves us the same way the Father loves Him. Do you realize how loved you really are?

> "
> *You cannot exhaust His love. He doesn't get tired of loving you.*
> "

In the Gospel of John, the author (John) never mentions his name in the entire book. Instead, he calls himself "the disciple whom Jesus loved." Isn't that cool? He didn't say "the disciple who loved Jesus so much" or "the awesome apostle." John knew God's love for him, and he made it his identity. His identity wasn't in his love for God, his profession, or any label the world could offer; his identity was found in God's love for him.

Try that out next time you meet someone new. Instead of saying something like, "I'm John, and I'm a businessman" or "I'm Lisa, and I'm a housewife and mother of three" try saying "I'm John (or Lisa), the one whom Jesus loves."

Hearing God's Opinion

"Hey, beloved, I'm madly in love with you. I'll never be mad at you. I promise. Nothing you or anyone else does can tear My love away from you. My love for you is unshakeable. It's My passion to love you. I care for you, and I promise that no matter what you face or go through, I'll be there with you to comfort and remind you that no matter what happens, I'm fully devoted to you."

Delighted In

*"The L*ORD* your God is in your midst;*

he is a warrior who can deliver.

He takes great delight in you; he renews you by his love;

he shouts for joy over you."

Zephaniah 3:17 NET

I don't have children, but my little brother was born when I was seventeen, so I got to experience some of the things parents do. I remember the love I felt when little Christian first came home. It was like nothing I'd felt before. I didn't realize I could love someone like that.

Everything he did was cute. Everything new he did was such a proud moment for me. To see him roll over the first time, or to hear him talk in baby gibberish, was like watching him win the Olympics. Every moment was an adventure with him. I was so excited to see what he would do next.

Next thing I knew, Christian started crawling and standing. I knew the day would soon come when he would walk—which, if you didn't know, is like the Super Bowl for babies. These little guys train so hard for that moment.

I remember his first step like it was yesterday. Christian stood, looked at my mom, then stepped forward like Neil Armstrong on the moon. Almost immediately, he fell—right into my mom's embrace. In that moment, my whole family delighted in Christian. We celebrated his success and loved on him so much.

As he continued learning to walk, we of course didn't yell or get mad at him whenever he fell. We delighted in every step he took, and when he fell, we tried to be there to catch him every time.

In our lives as Christians, we often think that when we fall, God is mad at us or yelling at us for messing up. But the good news of Jesus is that He took away our missteps and He's

there to catch us when we fall. He loves being there for us. He
loves comforting us and assuring us in every moment.

> "He'll never get tired of being there when we fall."

He'll never get tired of being there when we fall.

Maybe Christian's story isn't your story. It wasn't always mine either, as I was growing up. I always thought I was in trouble, even when I knew I wasn't. I lived in fear of messing up. I always felt I wasn't doing enough, and I could never relax because there was always something more I could do. I have scars; we all do. But the beauty of God is that He uses our scars to show us the goodness of His Son. He works everything for our good. Even the messy things.

Maybe you never heard your dad or mom say they were proud of you, or that they liked you or were pleased with who you are. That creates a scar. Whether we realize it or not, we often see God in a similar way we see our parents. If our parents were mad and grumpy, we tend to think that's how God is too.

The Bible says that if we want to know what God the Father is like, we look to Jesus. And Jesus loved us so much that He gave His life for us. Take a moment to let that sink in.

God is crazy about you. He was eternally satisfied before He created you and me. And why did He create us? To love us. To show us the riches of His goodness. Sure, God doesn't like when we sin, because it hurts us. But He's not mad, nor does He leave us. Instead, He's always with us and always delighting in us, in every step we take in dependence on Him.

In your every mistake, God is with you. He doesn't run off when you mess up, then ask you to work your way back to Him. No, He enters the mess with you and reminds you, "I'm here, I love you, and we'll get through this together."

> "
> In your every mistake,
> God is with you.
> "

Jesus got mad at sin on the cross. He took it upon Himself, then He took it away forever. He remembers our sin no more. This is why He can delight in us in every moment. He knows we won't walk perfectly, and that's okay with Him; He's not in a rush for you to behave perfectly. He just loves you, and He loves to delight in you.

Hearing God's Opinion

"What I did for you through the cross and resurrection was enough. This means nothing you do can change our relationship. We're good to go. It's such an adventure living inside of you! I love every moment with you. Look up, child! See My delight in you. I promise to work every mistake you make for your good. I'm never tired of you, and you never irritate Me. Enjoy Me enjoying you."

Qualified

And He has qualified us as ministers of a new covenant.

2 Corinthians 3:6 BSB

Obedient, moral, and *faithful.* These are the words the Bible uses to describe Abraham. If you grew up in church, you probably heard how Abraham was so obedient that he was willing to sacrifice his son. You heard about his spotless behavior and his unwavering trust in God.

Unfaithful, liar, and *idolater.* These words actually describe Abraham at different points in his life. When God meets and calls Abraham, he's worshiping other gods.

What I love is that God doesn't choose someone who has it all together. He doesn't choose the best dressed or the one with straight A's. He chooses the most unlikely people to change the world.

It gets better. Before Abraham does anything good or godly, God makes promises to give him land, to make his descendants into a vast nation, and to bless the world through him. The rest of the Old Testament is rooted in this promise of God to Abraham, a promise based not on Abraham's commitment to God, but on God's commitment to him.

God didn't use Abraham because he was qualified or did a bunch of good things. Out of His kindness, God called Abraham and gave him an identity apart from what Abraham did or didn't do. Abraham was qualified because of God, not because his actions were good.

After God calls Abraham, Abraham flees. He lies to others about his wife, saying she's his sister. Instead of trusting God to provide a son, he takes his servant and fathers a son through her. Then he lies again about his wife.

So what's the point? You don't have to behave perfectly

to be used by God. That's the good news of Abraham's story.

Your current sin or past mistakes don't disqualify you from being loved or used by God. God's promises to us

"
Your current sin or past mistakes don't disqualify you from being loved or used by God.
"

don't rest on our performance or our faithfulness to God, but on His faithfulness to us. The identity He gives us isn't affected by what we do. And God's ability to use us isn't blocked by our mistakes.

When the New Testament writers talk about Abraham, they don't bring up his mistakes; they talk about how God used him. They call Abraham righteous and obedient, and they even say he never weakened in faith. The same is true of God. He never defines us by our sin. God doesn't root our identity in our failures; it's always in what He has done for us. God has anointed us, qualified us, and made us His instruments apart from anything we do.

He's looking to use you in incredible ways. You're qualified to minister Jesus and be used by Jesus in every way. And you're one choice away from letting Christ in you express

Himself through you to everyone around you.

Although we hear this, many of us still think our past or the labels we've been given prevent us from being used by God. But think of Rahab, who's known in the Bible as "the prostitute." This was her profession. She was used and abused by men every day. Dirty. Unwanted. Unloved.

One night she encounters spies who've come to check out her city. Out of desperation to be accepted and utilized, she hides the spies. If she's found out, she'll be killed. The men escape, take the land, and Rahab the prostitute finds a man who loves her.

Rahab's descendant (almost thirty generations later) is our Savior, Jesus Christ. No longer known for what she did, Rahab is now known for the family she's a part of. From the lineage of Rahab the prostitute came the flawless, perfect Son of God.

You're not qualified because of what you do or what you've done. God alone qualifies you. So isn't it time to stop listening to your past and start listening to God's opinion of you?

There's nothing wrong with you. There's nothing you've done or will do that will make God stop using you. And there's nothing you can do to change God's mind about you. You're not in God's way; you're not an obstacle. You're qualified and equipped to be radically used by God to love those around you.

> "
> *There's nothing you can do to change God's mind about you.*
> "

Hearing God's Opinion

"I've enabled you and permanently qualified you to show people who I am. You're so unique, and you're such a gift to everyone around you. I don't need you to be like anyone else. Your voice, talents, and ability are perfect. Nothing will prevent Me from using you. You can trust yourself."

8

Wonderfully Made

I will praise you, because I have been remarkably

and wondrously made.

Psalm 139:14 CSB

Is there anything better than Amazon Prime? One click, and boom, your package is delivered. I can barely get to the door before I hear a knock from the UPS guy.

I recently ordered some shoes online for the first time, and I was so eager to get them. I was pumped. I rushed home from work, and there it was at my door, the Amazon box. I picked it up and rushed inside, grabbed my knife, opened the box, and—nothing. It was empty.

Throwing the box down in disgust, I thought,

This box is worthless!

Just as I was throwing a temper tantrum (I still do that; don't judge me), I heard a knock at the door. It was the UPS man with a box in his hand. Shoes inside. Apparently, someone had left an old box on my front step. Who knew?

Here's the thing. That Amazon box is worthless apart from what it carries inside. I learned that the hard way. But when the Amazon box has something inside, the box takes on the value of what it carries. The box is made to carry something. That's its purpose.

That's the question many of us ask: What's my purpose?

Just like the box, apart from Christ, we don't have much purpose. We're empty and lifeless. But the good news is, as believers we're never apart from Christ. And Christ is always in us. In Him, we've been wonderfully made, and we now have great value and worth.

> "
> The good news is, as believers we're never apart from Christ.
> "

Our purpose is to have Christ in us. And since we have Him, we're now able to be used in incredible ways. Not only that, but we're able to know Christ intimately since He lives in us. God created us to have relationship with Him. The purpose and goal of our life is to know Jesus. And knowing Jesus changes everything.

What is our worth? God says we're worth *Jesus* to Him. He didn't need us, but He wanted us—so much so that He sent His Son to rescue us and then infuse us with His own life. Do you realize that Christ lives in you? That may sound far-fetched, but if you believe in Jesus, then He lives inside all that you call *you*.

What I'm most thankful for is this: Even when we were a box without purpose, Jesus came and died for us. He came to give us meaning and value and love. He didn't throw us aside or give up on us; He pursued us and saved us. He didn't pick us up and throw us aside and say, "Worthless." Instead, He saw us, loved us, picked us up, and gave us infinite worth. He now looks at us and says, "Worthy and wonderfully made." And because of that, He wants to use you. You're His instrument.

I struggle with wanting to get my worth from what people say about me. I long to be affirmed in everything I do. It feels good. But the thing I keep learning is that affirmation and worth from others fades fast.

Growing up, I pursued my worth in what girls thought about me. I went from one girl and relationship to the next. They never satisfied. If anything, I felt worse. I felt worthless. Whether I was accepted or rejected, it didn't matter; nothing made me feel worthy. I was always having to do something to be worthy or feel worthy.

The beautiful thing about God is that He declares us worthy long before we do anything for Him. God's affirmation of our worth never fades. And it's the only thing that will ever satisfy our need to be known and affirmed.

God's not asking us to do things in order to be worthy. He's asking us to live out of the worth He has given us. In everything we do, we can know we have all the value we need in Him.

> "
> *God's not asking us to do things in order to be worthy. He's asking us to live out of the worth He has given us.*
> "

I once heard a story of a speaker who held up a hundred-dollar bill before an audience and asked, "Who would like this?" Of course, everyone in the crowd raised their hand.

Then he proceeded to crumple the hundred-dollar bill in his hand. He then asked, "Who still wants it?" All the hands raised again. He then threw the bill on the floor and stomped on it and ground it with his shoe. He picked up the bill and asked, "Who still wants it?" All the hands again raised. You see, none of that abuse altered the value of that bill; its worth didn't change based on what it had been through.

The same is true of us. No matter our thoughts, our sins, or what others might think, our value and worth are unchanging.

God is passionate about healing our hurts. He's freed us from the damage and hurt that we've gone through, and He's working to show us how He is enough in our hurt. I've had people I love call me things that no one should every be called. I always thought that because of that, I was damaged goods. I thought the real me didn't deserve love. That's why I was so good at faking it and wearing a mask around people.

I always believed that if people knew who I was, they wouldn't like it and would treat me poorly. But what I've come to discover is, the real me is flawless. And although my pain and hurt is real, God's grace and healing are just as real. No abuse or hurt can change the meaning and value God has given me—or you.

"
No abuse or hurt can change the meaning and value God has given me—or you.
"

We're brand new. Nothing can change that. We're made in God's image. This means we look like God—and if He likes what He sees, who are we to disagree?

When God created the entire earth and universe, He called it good. But when God created humanity, He called us *very* good. You're not just *good* in God's eyes; you're *very good*. So ditch the lie that says you're bad, wicked, or dirty, and embrace the truth that you are very good!

Hearing God's Opinion

"I took My time with you. And I didn't get anything wrong. You're My most prized possession. I know you've heard some stuff, and maybe you've believed lies about your body, self, or personality. But what I say about you is enough. I know that you may never perfectly believe or feel wonderfully made, and that's okay. But you can know that I'm no liar, and you, child, are beautifully and wonderfully made."

Blameless

Now to Him who is able to keep you from stumbling,

and to make you stand in the presence of His glory

blameless with great joy.

Jude 24

When I was in the fifth grade, I thought I was the coolest kid in school. In my class of about thirty kids, I thought I ruled the roost. I was the class clown, and was always in trouble for talking out and being a smart mouth. (Not much has changed.)

My teacher threatened me with all sorts of punishment: taking away my recess, calling my parents, sending me to the principal. Nothing seemed to work. Then one day after I'd again done something to drive my teacher insane, he said, "Zach, that one is going on your record forever."

Wait—what? My record? Will I ever be able to get a job? Or go to college? Or finish fifth grade?

From that day forward, the way my teacher tried to get me to behave was to threaten me with my record. He hung that over my head, trying to use fear to motivate me.

Most of us live our lives thinking God is keeping score or keeping a record. We think one day we'll hit heaven and He'll pull out our record of sins and begin punishing us or embarrassing us for them.

Guess what? The record has been canceled. Torn up. There is no record. Jesus became our sin and took away our sins so that we would never face judgment for them. That's the good news of the cross. In Christ, we've been freed from judgment. The judgment for our sin was death. Jesus took our sin and the judgment for it by dying. And the conclusion is that we no longer have to face punishment for our sin, since the punishment was taken by Jesus on our behalf.

We can confidently know that God chooses not to hold our sins against us. Jesus won't refer to them when He comes back. And we can wake up and fall asleep each day knowing that God will never,

> "Since God is love, He's not keeping a record of your wrongs."

ever judge us for our sins. Since God is love, He's not keeping a record of your wrongs.

I'm twenty-five, and I've never seen that record my teacher threatened me with. Nor did my teacher have much success improving my behavior through threats.

God doesn't threaten us, condemn us, or shame us for our sin. Instead, He teaches, comforts, and secures us in every moment. He doesn't motivate us to behave by fear, but by His love. He isn't writing down your failures; instead, He's with you in the midst of your failures, saying, "You're free, and no one can blame you."

Jesus walked into our classroom, took the record of every bad thing we've done, looked at the teacher, and tore that record up. And just because Jesus is good, He took His record, gave it to us, and said, "My perfect record is now yours."

God is not up in heaven writing down everything you do wrong. No, Love keeps no record of wrongs. God is living in your heart, reminding you of everything He did right for you and to you.

"
God is living in your heart, reminding you of everything He did right for you and to you.
"

Hearing God's Opinion

"I'm not keeping track of what you do. Remember, I keep no record of your mistakes—not now or ever. There's no catch. I've chosen to forget your sins forever. There'll be days when you feel accused and blamed, but that's not from Me! I'll never motivate you by shaming you or guilting you. I'll never make you feel bad for something you did wrong. Look to Me; look at My nail-pierced hands. I did it all for you. And it worked. You don't have to fear punishment anymore. I love you more than you'll ever know!"

10

United

But the one who joins himself to the Lord

is one spirit with Him.

1 Corinthians 6:17

The star of every wedding is the bride. But as a pastor, I get a close up of someone else: the groom.

Have you seen the eyes of the groom when he first sees his bride? Tears, excitement, awe. When you look into the groom's eyes, all you see is the bride. You see why he loves her and why they're both here.

Have you looked into the eyes of Jesus? They're filled with inexhaustible love.

> "
> Have you looked into the eyes of Jesus? They're filled with inexhaustible love.
> "

Take a deeper look, and you'll see a bride—pure, set apart, and perfect. You are that bride. He cannot live without you. Which is why He decided to marry us, to unite Himself with our spirit, promising never to leave us or forsake us.

In marriage, the bride gets a new name, a new home, and a new family. The same is true for us. God gives us His name. He makes us His home. And He welcomes us into His family forever.

The Bible says that our relationship with Jesus is just like marriage. We become united with Jesus. Our spirit and His Spirit are joined. This is how He lives in us. We're inseparable. We're close, near, together. Religious people speak of "getting closer to God," but the Bible never uses these terms. Instead we see that we *are* close, together, near, united, and one.

Sure, we're learning about Jesus, but we're not getting closer to Him in proximity. We don't have to work hard to somehow get close to God. Nor do we lose our spot when we mess up. He lives in us all the time, no matter what. This means He hears our every cry and prayer.

God is not off in heaven asking us to work our way to Him. Instead, He's in our heart reminding us that He worked His way to us. It was His work that made us close, not ours.

" It was His work that made us close, not ours. "

***

A widow. Ungodly. Foreigner. Unclean woman. This is Ruth. She goes to a foreign land with her mother-in-law to work and survive. She thinks the rest of her life will be spent looking for scraps and being an outsider.

Godly. Pure. Full of honor. This is Boaz. He's a landowner. One day he stumbles on this woman named Ruth who's working on his land. He's kind to her and gives her food to eat and allows her to keep coming back for more.

In that day, a kinsman-redeemer was one who could marry or help one of his relatives. Boaz became that for Ruth, who proposed to marry Boaz. She did this by going to lie at his feet in the middle of the night.

According to the tradition of the day, Boaz shouldn't marry a foreigner. He shouldn't marry someone unclean. He shouldn't marry someone who was ungodly. This wouldn't be good for his business or his name. It was reckless.

But Boaz married Ruth—not because of what she offered him or could do for him, but because of his love for her.

In the same way, God our Redeemer did not save us and unite Himself to us because of what we could do for Him. God simply wants relationship with us. That's it. There's no catch. Ruth didn't have to

" *God simply wants relationship with us. That's it. There's no catch.* "

earn or deserve Boaz's love. She became married because of his love for her. The same is true for you and me with God.

In the Old Testament, God dwelt in a place called the Holy of Holies. No normal person could enter this place, because God's holiness would kill them. Once a year a priest could enter after being purified and washed through the ceremonial requirements. And that was it. Why? God can live only in set-apart, perfect places.

In the New Testament, God dwells in you, the holy of holies. The perfect place. If the God of the universe is united to you, what does that say about you?

Hearing God's Opinion

"You should hear and see what people say about us. They love our expression. Each time you let Me express Myself through you—people go crazy. You and I are so compatible. I'm closer than you know. No matter what you go through, I'm with you in it all. I can't wait for you to experience all that I have for you. No matter what you choose, I'm united to you. You're free to do what you want, knowing My will for you is to trust Me in every moment."

11

Masterpiece

For we are God's masterpiece.

He has created us anew in Christ Jesus,

so we can do the good things he planned for us long ago.

Ephesians 2:10 NLT

In an experiment a number of years ago, a psychologist put large realistic scars on the faces of a group of people, then told them to go out to see how the public reacted to them.[2] However, before they were sent out, the participants were told that some last-minute touch-ups were required on their scars. During these touch-ups, the scars were actually removed

2   Sandra Blakesley, "How You See Yourself: Potential for Big Problems," The New York Times, February 7, 1991, https://www.nytimes.com/1991/02/07/news/how-you-see-yourself-potential-for-big-problems.html

without the subjects knowing it; they still thought they wore scars as they went out in public.

After returning, they all reported the same experience: people were mean to them, looked at them weird, and were judgmental. Their mistaken self-view affected how they thought others saw them—which consequently affected how they saw themselves.

Most of us live as if we have scars. We live as if what Jesus did on the cross made no difference. Do you have past scars that define you? Do you hold on to labels that people have given you? Do you see yourself the way God sees you, or do you think something's uniquely wrong with you?

The good news is that Jesus has made you new. He has taken your mess and turned it into a masterpiece. He has taken your scars and redeemed them. He has ripped off the labels the world has given you and has given you a new label—*masterpiece*.

> "
> He has taken your mess and turned it into a masterpiece.
> "

You're His finest work. Nothing you've done defines you. Nothing you'll do can define you. God is the only One who defines you. And He says, "You are my finest work, my masterpiece, my favorite."

I'm a guy, but I struggle with how I look. Some think that's only a girl thing, but it isn't. The body image thing, I get it. The struggle is real. The mirror is a liar. Comparison is a thief. Here's what I've learned: When you look in the mirror, choose to see yourself the way God does. He created us, and if He's good with how we look, then you and I are good.

Our identity doesn't come from how we feel about ourselves. Nor does it come from what the scale says, what a paycheck says, or what anyone says. Our identity is rooted in Christ *alone*.

God doesn't make mistakes; He makes masterpieces. You're not a mistake. God didn't mess up when He created you. He likes everything about you. We can hear this message, but we still get thoughts every day that tell us we're a mistake and a mess. The good news: We can choose not to entertain those thoughts. We can choose not to compare. Sure, we may struggle with this; everyone does. But we still have the power to choose between God's thoughts or negative thoughts.

It's not your fault that you get the thoughts. It's crucial to understand that the thoughts do not come from us; they come from sin and shame. Although shame often speaks in the first person, we're not our shame.

The world is a mess. Your thoughts and behavior are a mess. But you, the child of God, are not a mess. You're God's masterpiece, no matter what you think, feel, or do.

"You, the child of God, are not a mess. You're God's masterpiece, no matter what you think, feel, or do."

The voice living in you is greater than the voice that's in the world. You're not bound to what you've heard or what you've done. Jesus sees you as perfect and good because he has actually made you this way. He doesn't call you a masterpiece just to make you feel good. He calls you a masterpiece because that's who you are. And God is no liar. So you don't need to fix or improve yourself. Instead, learn who you are and start being yourself.

Our job is not to fix our behavior or fix the sin we struggle with. Instead, we're called to live from our identity and trust Jesus. The fruit of trusting Jesus and living from who we are in Him is that our behavior begins to reflect who we are, and the sin we most struggle with begins to lose power. We may be acting and living one way, but no matter what, we're still God's masterpiece.

Think about the caterpillar and the butterfly. If you were to look on the inside of the caterpillar, it would have the same makeup as a butterfly. It looks like something it's not. Its core identity is a butterfly, and one day it will outwardly exhibit what's true on the inside. The same is true of us. *Masterpiece* is our core identity, and God is revealing to us who we are on the inside and inviting us to live from that reality. The behavior and actions will display naturally when we live from who we are.

You're special to God. His favorite. He loves living in you. He thinks you're His best creation. God could have chosen to live anywhere else, but He chose to live in you.

> "
> God could have chosen to live anywhere else, but He chose to live in you.
> "

Hearing God's Opinion

"Do you know how valuable you are? I gave My life to you because that's how much you're worth to Me. You're My most valued treasure. There's nothing about you that's bad. I'm not trying to change you. I already did that at salvation. My goal for you is to realize who I've made you. I love how you look, and I love who you are. You are My masterpiece."

12

Flawless

For by one offering He has perfected for all time
those who are sanctified.

Hebrews 10:14

The Bible tells a story about an unclean woman. She's an outcast. According to the law in her culture, she cannot touch or be touched by anyone. She's tried for years to get better, visiting every doctor and doing everything medically possible, but nothing has worked.

Then one day, she touches Jesus. According to the law at the time, it's a sin and a crime for her to do this. But what happens?

She's healed.

That's the good news of Jesus: He makes you clean. Just like you don't clean yourself up before you jump in the shower. You just jump in and the shower cleans you. In the same way, you don't clean yourself before you come to Jesus. You go to Jesus in order to get clean.

After this woman touched Him, Jesus turned around to look for her. This was not in order to accuse or condemn her. Jesus looked for her so He could love her, heal her, and save her.

This woman was scared to death. She didn't know what Jesus would do if He found out she'd touched Him. Like many of us, this woman thought God was mad at her. But when Jesus saw her, He didn't call her by any label the world put on her. Jesus said, "Daughter." She was no longer an unclean woman; she was a daughter of the King. It would have been enough if Jesus just healed her, but He did more. He gave her a new name.

Holy. Righteous. Blameless. Everything we say about Jesus, He says about us. That's why we're children of God. We now carry His name.

We often think that our past makes us impure. We think God sees us as flawed and worthless. But the truth is that the moment Jesus touched our lives, we became forever pure. Totally flawless. Perfect.

> "
> *The truth is that the moment Jesus touched our lives, we became forever pure. Totally flawless. Perfect.*
> "

This identity isn't changed or altered by what we've done or where we've been. Although we may act imperfectly, our identity as flawless stays the same. Jesus gives us our identity; the world and our behavior do not.

Here's the thing. My past is littered with regret and mistakes that I desperately wish I could take back. I've been in unhealthy relationships, and I've done things that aren't meant to be done outside marriage. In the eyes of most Christians (and people in the world), I'm not pure. Maybe you can relate.

The good news is that you and I—we—are pure. We're clean. We're perfect. Sure, it doesn't feel that way. But the truth is the truth, no matter what you and I feel. And those who think they're pure because of something they do are wrong.

The Bible says that thinking impurely is the same as

acting impurely. We're all in the same boat, which is why we need purity as a gift, not as something we achieve. Put another way, purity and our entire identity are received, not achieved.

"*Purity and our entire identity are received, not achieved.*"

The old, impure me with all my past sins was crucified and buried with Christ, and the new Zach who is pure and clean was raised to new life in Jesus. The same is true of you.

God isn't pretending to see us this way. This is who we really are. He has taken our past and redeemed it. He promises to work all the mistakes for our good. And He's not holding our sins against us. Although our past may have brought us hurt, God's presence in us brings healing. His label for us is *daughter, son, clean, faultless.*

Maybe you think, *That doesn't sound humble—to say we're perfect.* Sure, we still mess up, but remember, God has given us our identity apart from what we do. For example, if I choose to act like a chicken, it doesn't mean I'm a chicken. I'm a human who is acting like a chicken. I'm still human. Perfect is now our identity at the core. When we choose to sin, we're perfect children of God who are sinning. But we're still perfect. I'm not claiming that I act perfectly; I'm saying I've been made perfect forever by Jesus.

True humility is agreeing with what God says, no matter your feelings. True humility is saying the same thing God says about you. If God says you're perfect, who are you to disagree? That's what it means to walk by faith and not sight. Walking by faith is trusting who God says you are, even if you can't see it.

> "
> *If God says you're perfect, who are you to disagree?*
> "

Hearing God's Opinion

"Nothing compares to you. You're perfect. I find no flaw in you. I know it's hard to believe that, because you still mess up. You still get thoughts and feelings that tell you you're a mistake, or you're flawed. But what I'm saying is real. Because of what I've done for you, you're forever perfect."

13

Blessed

Praise be to the God and Father of our Lord Jesus Christ,
who has blessed us in the heavenly realms
with every spiritual blessing in Christ.
Ephesians 1:3 NIV

Santa Claus is a thug. I mean, really. He sits on his throne all year, judges kids, then hands out gifts to those who are good and lumps of coal to those who are bad.

I hated that picture growing up, because I was the bad kid. But I'm also an optimist, so I used the coal and had a barbecue.

Santa is also creepy. Did you know he watches you when you sleep? I don't know about you, but I don't want an old man watching me when I sleep.

When I was growing up, Santa resembled God to me. I thought God sat on His throne judging whether we were good or bad. And maybe if we were good enough, He would gift us or bless us with something. What I didn't realize was that Santa operated out of karma. And I thought God did too. That's why I thought God was always mad at me and ready to hurl coal my way. I don't know about you, but I don't behave perfectly.

But God is not Santa (which is some of the best news I've ever heard). If you're a Christmas fanatic, I'm sorry to burst your bubble, but God is way better than Santa. Whereas Santa operates out of karma, God operates out of grace.

Karma means you get what you deserve. But God's grace means you get what Jesus deserves. That's the scandal of Christianity. No one is good, and we all deserve death. But Jesus came and took what we deserved so we could get what He deserved forever.

> "
> *Jesus came and took what we deserved so we could get what He deserved forever.*
> "

Religion is a lot like Santa. You work hard for the blessing, and if you're good enough, you get the gift. But Jesus isn't like Santa. On day one of our salvation, He blesses us with everything heaven has to offer. The Bible never says, "God will bless you if …" The Bible says God has already blessed us with every spiritual blessing.

We live from His blessings, not for them.

That's why we live from His blessings, not for them.

It's no longer about being good enough. Instead it's about trusting in the One who is good. We aren't motivated by fear of being punished. Instead, we're motivated by God's outrageous grace that He has lavished on us.

While Santa is far off at the North Pole and visits only once a year, Jesus is near, living in your heart, and He promises to never leave you. Santa checks his list in order to bless you. Jesus destroyed the list and has blessed us apart from what we do.

Because Jesus was cursed on the cross, you are always blessed. His attitude toward you will never waver. Next time your circumstances aren't pleasant, know that they aren't from God. He's in you, reminding you that everything you need, you already have in Him.

For many of us, this is difficult to fathom. We're used to getting what we deserve. We're used to working really hard or being really good and hopefully being rewarded or catching a break. But Christianity isn't like that. God isn't looking for our best effort; He wants our trust. We're not waiting and hoping for God to give us something; instead we're living from all that He has already given us.

This concept changed everything for me. I thought that if I could read my Bible a little more, obey a little more, or just be good a little more, then things would start going my way. Maybe my circumstances would get better. Or if I had more faith, then my situation would change. Many of us think we can earn God's blessings. Or if we're good enough, He'll bless us or do something for us. But the good news is that Jesus did everything to earn God's blessing for us.

When I realized that everything I need I already have, I stopped trying to get God to fix my circumstances through my good behavior. Instead I started enjoying God in the midst of my circumstances. Jesus doesn't promise us good circumstances. He actually says that we'll face trouble. But He also promises to be life and peace to us in the midst of everything this world brings us.

Like the apostle Paul, we can be content in either poverty or plenty, sickness or health, because Christ really is enough for us. Jesus is calling us to live our lives from all that He is within us. God is for us, and God is good. He doesn't cause all things, but He does cause all things to work for our good.

He doesn't cause all things, but He does cause all things to work for our good.

The next time a bad circumstance hits, how would it look to realize you are blessed? We don't need to obey more or serve more or do more for God to bless us. No, He has given us all heaven has to offer in His Son Jesus Christ. And He lives in you every moment.

Because of what Jesus has done on our behalf, we never have to wonder if God is cursing us or hurling disaster our way. God operates out of grace, and He can only be for us and good to us.

Hearing God's Opinion

"I took all your sin so you never have to doubt My goodness toward you. I'll always be gracious to you, no matter what. My grace will keep you firm in the midst of any circumstance you face. I'm faithful, and I promise to comfort you in all your affliction. I've established you in My love, and I've given you the very best of heaven— My Son, Jesus Christ. Now go, enjoy the riches of the spiritual blessings I've already freely given you."

14

Saved

For it is by grace you have been saved, through faith—and this is

not from yourselves, it is the gift of God—not by works,

so that no one can boast.

Ephesians 2:8–9 NIV

"Dad, I know you're not dead, but can I get my inheritance?"

"Umm ... sure, son."

So the prodigal son took his inheritance and ran off to another country. He spent all his money living a wild life. After he was broke and had nothing, a famine happened. What did he do? He got a job feeding pigs.

But he still was hungry, and no one gave him anything

to eat. After the son had smelled enough pig stuff, he remembered how well-fed his father's servants always were—while here he was, starving. So the son decided to go back to the father. He planned an elaborate apology to persuade his father to accept him back, and he headed home hoping just to be a servant.

But while he was a long way off, the father saw him coming—then ran to him, hugged him, and kissed him.

The father didn't ask where the son had been. He didn't ask the son for an apology or for ten reasons why he should welcome him back. No, the father got him new clothes, his debit card, and some new Jordans. Not only that, but the father threw him a party with the finest steaks, wings, and burgers around.

The father didn't condemn the son; he celebrated him.

God saved us by His kindness and goodness, not by our effort or work. There's nothing we could do to save ourselves. God pursued us, found us, and then saved us. It was God's pursuit of us, not our pursuit of God, that saved us. It's by God's grace, not our goodness, that we're saved. Grace is God's radical pursuit of us in kindness and love. We're saved by Jesus's work on our behalf, not by any work we can do.

"
We're saved by Jesus's work on our behalf, not by any work we can do.
"

That's why anyone who says yes to Jesus as Lord will be saved. That's it. All God wants us to do is to believe that Jesus is Lord and was raised from the dead: "Jesus, I believe You're my Lord and Savior, I believe You rose from the dead, and I want You to be my everything."

God didn't save you to make you His servant. God saved you to celebrate you. He saved you to lavish you with His kindness. He's not asking you to live your life trying to repay the grace He has lavished on you; He's asking you to live your life enjoying that grace!

"
He's not asking you to live your life trying to repay the grace He has lavished on you; He's asking you to live your life enjoying that grace!
"

There was nothing you could do to earn your salvation. And there's nothing you can do to work yourself out of it. Your salvation is a fact, not a feeling. And it involves more than just going to heaven when you die. The Bible says that eternal life starts now.

Think about it. What makes heaven so great? *Jesus.* And Jesus lives in you today, which means we can enjoy Him in every moment.

No matter what you've done or what you do, Jesus doesn't regret saving you. There'll never be an instance when He lets you go. Nothing can take you from His hand or revoke your place in heaven. Your sin doesn't surprise God; He has seen it all, and He chooses to love you and be for you forever.

He'll never get tired of being your Savior. He'll never get tired of living in you. He'll never get tired of *you.*

Hearing God's Opinion

"Rest in all that I've already done. I've finished the work. There's nothing wrong with our relationship. We have peace. I adore you. Do you hear it? My Spirit is witnessing with yours that you're My child! You're the one I went to the cross for. Continue to live your life in the same way that you received Me. Trust Me. Let Me take your burdens. No matter what sin you commit, you'll always be Mine. You're locked in for good. I promise that nothing can take you away from Me. You're saved completely and forever."

15

Free

*It is for freedom that Christ has set us free. Stand firm, then,
and do not let yourselves be burdened again by a yoke of slavery.*
Galatians 5:1 NIV

Smack! My face hit the water for the fifth time, and I was tired of wakeboarding. I'd watched my brother-in-law Calen wakeboard hundreds of times, and I knew I could do it. He would do flips off the wake and jump higher than the boat, so I thought surely I could at least stand up. (If you don't know, a wakeboard is a board with boots on it. You strap your feet in, hold a rope, and the boat pulls you as you ride along on this board.)

I couldn't even ride. The moment the boat moved, I would stand and then fall and drink a mouthful of water.

Calen kept telling me, "You almost got it! Just let the boat pull you up." The problem was that I was tugging too hard on the rope. I was trying my best to pull myself up. But my effort wasn't working.

After about the millionth time, I was so exhausted that I just let the boat pull me up—and I started wakeboarding. It wasn't a perfect ride, and I fell down a lot. And if we went wakeboarding today, you'd realize I'm still not that good at it. Sometimes I still think I can pull myself up. But each time I try, I realize it won't work. There's only one way: let the boat do the work.

Christianity is about trusting, not trying. The more we try to be led by the Spirit

"
Christianity is about trusting, not trying.
"

or live the Christian life by our own effort, the more we fail. Jesus is calling us to simply let Him lead us and pull us up.

He is the source. He is the strength. He is the power and the life that moves us. He isn't giving us laws to lead us; instead, He's asking us to trust in His lead. That's true freedom. True freedom is living dependently on Jesus, knowing He'll never lead you to slavery again.

When Jesus lived on earth, He was completely free and yet completely dependent on the Father at the same time. He was perfectly righteous and perfectly dependent. The same is true of us. Our dependency doesn't limit our freedom; instead, our dependency leads us into what we really want, which is true freedom.

The law says, "Try." But Jesus says, "Trust." That's the difference between the old covenant and the new. The law could tell you how to live, but had no power to enable you to live. The law enslaved us, but Jesus sets us free. And now He's simply inviting us to trust Him in everything.

The Christian life is not based on our determination and will power. It's not "do your part and then God will do His." No, the Christian life is God's work from start to finish. We're fully dependent upon Christ for everything. He's the source, He's our strength, and He's working in us and through us.

> "The Christian life is God's work from start to finish. "

We're free from living by rules and manipulation. This means we're free from the pressure of having to follow all the rules and keep them in fear of punishment. Instead, we just get to trust Jesus and follow His leading. Being led by the Spirit isn't about looking around and imitating a historical figure; it's about looking ahead and trusting the One who's leading you, the One who's alive in you today.

***

Have you ever been on a ropes course? They put you in a harness to keep you secure, then they let you go and walk on the obstacles and ropes. There's still the fear that the harness may not do its job and you'll fall to your death. (Or maybe that's just me.) Every time I slipped, I feared. But with every slip came the firm reminder that the harness was doing its job.

This is similar to our walk with Christ. He's our security. He's the harness that catches us when we slip, promising to never let go of us, no matter the slip. His grace is enough for every mistake we make. More than that, His grace is able to lead us and guide us into a godly life.

Here's the thing. The harness didn't make me want to slip and fall. No, the awareness that I was secure gave me confidence to walk on that tight rope without fear of death. The harness made me want to walk perfectly, not slip and fall. The same is true of God's grace. It doesn't make us want to abuse it, but to live from it by trusting Jesus.

That's what's so good about God's grace. He isn't punishing us when we fail; He's securing us and giving us the confidence to live life knowing that no matter what, we're safe, secure, and protected by Him.

You see, in this world, when we fail, we fall into rejection, punishment, and shame. But when we fail with God, we fall into His acceptance, love, and grace. We never fall into punishment or shame with Him.

> "
> *When we fail with God, we fall into His acceptance, love, and grace.*
> "

Jesus lives in your heart and has given you a new heart. He's asking you to simply live out of who you are. You're a new creation, with new desires; you're someone who no longer wants to sin. Yeah, that may be a shocker to you. But as a child of God, you'd rather do God things, not bad things. I know it doesn't always feel that way, but at your core, you want the same thing God wants. That's why God tells us to love and give and help others. He tells us these things because he knows they're the only things that will fulfill us.

This means we're not trying to become something we're not. We're not trying to do something God hasn't already equipped us to do. So instead of trying to become godly, simply trust that you already are. Instead of trying to live the Christian life, simply trust the Christ who is your life. Instead of trying to avoid sin, just trust in the One who'll never lead you to sin.

Just like my brother-in-law, each time you fall on your face, Jesus isn't yelling in disappointment. Instead, He's saying, "Just let Me do the work. I've got you. Let Me pull you up."

Hearing God's Opinion

"You cannot perfect your behavior by self-effort, rules, or anything you do. I've set you free from all that. Trust Me with it! You no longer have to submit to any form of slavery. You're called to live in the freedom of My goodness and love. I've given you everything you need to live a godly life. More than that, I've made you godly. You don't need a law to guide you. Just trust in My life to do what rules and laws could never do. I've got this. I've got you. Now live."

16

Never Punished

Therefore, there is now no condemnation
for those who are in Christ Jesus.

Romans 8:1 NIV

How does God react when we sin?

The woman gets thrown in front of this teacher, Jesus. Naked, embarrassed, and afraid, she looks around to see a crowd surrounding her. Not only is she buried in guilt over what she has done, but now everyone knows about it.

She hears a man ask this Jesus guy, "Should we stone her?"

She's been found out. She knows her story is done. She knows the law. Anyone caught in the act of adultery will be stoned to death.

Thud. Thud. Thud. One by one, she hears stones dropping, until everything is quiet. She looks up and sees Jesus. He asks, "Where are your accusers? Has no one condemned you?"

"No one, Lord."

"Neither do I condemn you. Go and sin no more."

The only One who could condemn us *became* sin for us, so that He could comfort us. Jesus will never condemn us, because He took all the condemnation for our sin. Jesus isn't about punishing us for our sin, but setting us free from our sin.

> " *Jesus isn't about punishing us for our sin, but setting us free from our sin.* "

It wasn't the woman's ability to live free from sin that caused Jesus to say, "Neither do I condemn you." No, His declaration that He would never punish her is what caused this woman to live free from sin.

Religion says, "Live sin-free, and God won't punish you." Jesus says, "Neither do I punish you; now go and live free from sin." God's declaration that we'll never be condemned doesn't cause us to take advantage of God's grace, but to celebrate it.

The same Jesus who spoke those words to the woman caught in adultery lives in your heart and is speaking those words to you when you sin. Since Jesus took away your sin, He's not shaming you when you mess up. Instead, He's reminding you that you're free, not condemned—and He loves you.

God will never, ever, ever punish you. He cannot punish you for your sins since they were punished and taken away at the cross. So how

> "
> God will never, ever, ever punish you.
> "

does God react when we sin? The Bible says that He silences our accusers, He picks us up and comforts us, He tells us that He'll never shame or punish us, and then He empowers us to go live free from sin.

No condemnation. Right now—not someday when we get our life together, and not just when we get to heaven. *Right now*, in every moment, there's no condemnation for those who believe in Jesus. No condemnation when you sin, and when you don't sin. This gift isn't based on what you do or don't do. It's a fact—something you can't get away from. It's irreversible.

No punishment for your sin is a promise from God based on His work, not yours.

Do you realize God treats you well? It's not that God is soft on sin. He took sin seriously, which is why He became sin on the cross. And it's not that God doesn't care about what we do. He hates when we sin, because it hurts us. It grieves Him. Just like a parent is grieved when their child touches a hot stove after being told not to.

God is grieved by our sin because He wants what's best for us. He wants us to walk after Him, not after sin, because He's the only way we'll be satisfied and free. But being grieved and being mad are two different things. You may suppose that it's humble to think God is mad and frustrated at us when we sin—but that thinking isn't biblical.

You need to know that God isn't mad at you. He's not disappointed with you. He's not irritated with your frequent mistakes. He'll never

He'll never grow tired of sustaining you and comforting you.

grow tired of sustaining you and comforting you.

So next time you sin, if the voice you hear is accusing, condemning, shaming, or guilting you, it isn't the voice of Jesus. Jesus is in the business of assuring us in the midst of accusation. Comforting us when we're feeling condemned. Silencing our shame. And giving us abundant grace for our guilt.

God is *for* you. You're always on His mind. There's never a moment when you don't have his full attention.

Hearing God's Opinion

"Please hear Me. I will never, ever punish you. You don't owe Me. You don't need to be afraid of Me. I took all the punishment for you. Now trust in the sufficiency of the cross. I'm your refuge, your safe place, the One in whom you can find safety and love. I promise you this: My kindness will never leave you."

17

Dead to Sin

So you also should consider yourselves
to be dead to the power of sin
and alive to God through Christ Jesus.

Romans 6:11 NLT

You may have heard how a circus elephant will stay in one place if it's simply roped to a little stake in the ground. How is that possible?

When the elephant is just a baby, the elephant trainers tie a rope around its neck and attach the rope to a sturdy stake planted firmly in the ground. The young elephant isn't quite strong enough to get free. It tries to break loose and walk away, but can't.

They do this each day, and the same thing always happens. The elephant realizes it cannot break free. It isn't strong enough. Eventually, the elephant becomes so used to this that only the rope is needed to keep the elephant from going anywhere. For the rest of its life, a small rope and a small stake in the ground are all it takes to hold back a full-grown elephant.

Sin once had us bound up. We couldn't muster enough effort or strength to set ourselves free from sin. That's why Jesus came and rescued us by stripping away the rope around our neck and giving us the power to live free from sin.

The struggle for many of us is that we've become so used to that rope around our neck, we don't realize it has no power. Like the full-grown elephant, we can believe the lie that we can't break free. Or we can realize that sin has no power over us anymore. We can walk away.

Many of us believe the lie that we're dirty, bad people. Often the message is that we're bad people trying to be good. But the message of the gospel is that we were dead and Jesus made us alive. Now we're good people who sometimes mess up.

Your life is not about trying to win the war over sin and death. Rather, your life is about daily trusting that Christ has already won that

> "Your life is about daily trusting that Christ has already won that war."

war. Jesus doesn't tell us to defeat sin; He invites us to rest in the victory over sin that He's already accomplished. Many of us have been sitting in the prison cell of sin, not realizing the door has been ripped off. Walk out. You're free!

When I realized who I am in Christ and what God thinks of me, I was set free from many different sins. That's what truth does. It always sets you free. The freedom I experienced didn't come from doing more or trying harder. It actually came from trusting in what Jesus did for me. It came from using the truth of His Word to combat the accusations and lies I'd heard and believed.

The only offensive weapon we have and need is the sword of the Spirit—God's Word. The Enemy says, "You're not enough." God's Word says, "I am in you, therefore you're enough." The Enemy says, "You are what you do." God's Word says, "You are what I have done for you." That's the crazy thing.

Satan knows who you are in Christ but chooses to define you by your mistakes. God knows all your mistakes but chooses to define you by who you are in Christ.

> " God knows all your mistakes but chooses to define you by who you are in Christ. "

The good news is that Jesus is in you. And His voice and presence have the power to influence and empower you. The Enemy is outside you and cannot touch you. Imagine yourself in a room with Jesus, and imagine the Enemy and sin being outside the room. You can see and hear the Enemy and sin. But can they touch you? No.

Further, whose voice is clearer—the one outside, or the one next to you? It's hard to listen to the voice of the accuser when we're focused on the voice of Jesus. When we fix our attention on Him, the things of this world fade into the background.

We're still going to struggle. None of us will ever live sinless in this life. But what Jesus has done for us and to us is real. True freedom from sin is our destiny as children of God.

I still struggle—a lot. But knowing my identity in

Christ has changed everything for me. I'm so fired up about the truth of who we are in Christ. Still, there are many days when I doubt, question, and struggle with sin. And that's okay. My struggle only means I need Jesus and I need to know who I am even more. My struggle doesn't make me an exception.

What I'm saying is not some formula you apply, and then boom, no more sinning. But truth does set us free. And the more time we spend with the truth of who we are, the more we begin living out of all that God says we are. The more we understand the good news of Jesus, the more we'll trust Him. That's the thing about spiritual growth in Christ. We don't grow more independent; instead, we grow more dependent on Jesus and what He says about us.

God has made you good and new. You now long to do the things that He wants. The freedom He gives you leads you from sin, not to sin. You want to love others and please God. It's who you are now. You're hardwired to live free from sin.

Hearing God's Opinion

"I've given you freedom. You're really free, no matter what you feel. Freedom is your destiny. I'm your strength in the midst of your struggles. I'm your victory in the midst of your sin. The truth is, you no longer want to sin. Look to Me! I promise to always give you a way out of temptation."

18

Forgiven

In him we have redemption through his blood,

the forgiveness of sins,

in accordance with the riches of God's grace.

Ephesians 1:7 NIV

One of the most popular stories in the Bible is that of David and Goliath—the young shepherd boy against the giant.

The Israelites are in a war with the Philistines. Except that no one is fighting. Each day, Goliath the giant steps forward and roars out the same challenge: the Israelites should send out a man for a one-on-one fight against him, and whoever wins that fight will win the war for his side, right then and there.

The Israelites, however, are not idiots; all of them are afraid to fight that brazen giant.

Enter David. He comes to the camp of Israel's army to deliver food from home for his older brothers. As he is delivering these things, he hears Goliath doing his daily routine—shouting, insulting, and challenging the Israelites. David can't believe his ears. To the Israelite soldiers nearby, he boldly speaks his utter contempt: "Who is this trash-talking giant to think he can get away with defying the armies of *the living God*?"

These words made quite an impression, and the boy gets summoned by Saul, Israel's king—before whom David immediately volunteers to fight Goliath. Saul knows that is impossible, but something about this shepherd boy makes the king willing to at least hear him out. After David testifies about killing lions and bears to protect his father's sheep, Saul accepts the boy's offer, and even lends his own armor to suit him up for the fight. But it's too big. And David wants only his slingshot.

One shot, and Goliath is dead. That's all it takes.

When I read this story, I don't think about being like

David—trying to be more courageous and bold and obedient. When I read this story, I think of Jesus. You see, if we're honest, we're the scared Israelites in that story, unwilling and unable to fight. They were hopeless. Jesus is David. And sin and death are represented by Goliath. Of course, this story is real, and it was significant for the history of Israel. But when we look back in the Old Testament, we so often see pictures and images of Christ. I believe this story is one of them.

Jesus, on our behalf, willingly takes on the impossible giant of sin and death, and defeats it once and for all. It takes Jesus only once to make us forgiven and free. We're forgiven of all our sins—past, present, and future—the moment we place faith in Christ.

> "We're forgiven of all our sins—past, present, and future—the moment we place faith in Christ."

Forgiven is who you are. It's part of your identity. There's not one moment you spend unforgiven. The Bible says that you're without blame and that God has forgotten your sins. How is this possible? Simple: what Jesus did for you worked the first time. There's no need for a repeat.

David didn't have to keep killing Goliath day after day. Once his stone struck Goliath, the deed was finished. Sound familiar? When Jesus defeated sin and death, he said, "It is finished", not, "More work needs to be done."

Guilt and shame are defeated. They have no power over you. They no longer define you.

***

I once heard a story about Thomas Edison, the guy who invented the light bulb. It took Edison and his team of men all day to create a bulb for testing. Finally, after that long day of work, Edison gave the bulb to a young intern to take upstairs for the test.

The boy took his time, making sure each step was slow and that he had a firm grasp on the bulb. Right as he got to the top step—crash! He dropped the bulb. Edison's team had to go back to work to recreate the bulb.

After another long day, the replacement bulb was ready. What did Edison do? He gave the new bulb to that young intern to carry upstairs.

The same is true of God. He doesn't hold our past mistakes against us. He forgets them and takes them

> "
> *He doesn't hold our past mistakes against us. He forgets them and takes them away.*
> "

away. Our sins don't stop Him from wanting to use us. He has limitless grace.

Edison didn't bring up the boy's mistake and condemn and shame him. No, Edison gave the bulb to the boy as if it was the first time.

God's forgiveness gives us confidence to see Him as good, and to know that He'll always be for us, no matter what. Our forgiveness enables us to focus our attention on Him, not on our past—and to move forward, knowing that all the work needed to make us forgiven has already been done by Jesus.

Hearing God's Opinion

"My blood was enough to take away your sins forever. I saw all your sins, and I've chosen to remove them as far as the east is from the west. Every sin you commit has been forgiven; there's no exception to My abundant grace. And I promise you, I'll never mention them again or hold them against you."

19

Like Jesus

This is how love is made complete among us
so that we will have confidence on the day of judgment:
In this world we are like Jesus.

1 John 4:17 NIV

Growing up in a small town in Texas meant that I loved football. The entire town shut down every Friday night, and everyone went to the game. Bright lights, food, and a pigskin—it all made for an awesome time. Thousands of people would show up early and stay late.

When I was in elementary school, our high school team was one of the best in the state. And the crowds who came for every game would come to particularly watch one dude: Jordan Shipley.

I wanted to be like Jordan. He was the fastest, smartest, best player on the field. I tried so hard to do what he did. To catch like Jordan caught, to run like Jordan ran. My highest goal was to one day be like him.

Many of us have heroes we look up to and want to be like. We see commercials of athletes or celebrities who we so desperately want to be. We then spend the rest of our lives trying to be like somebody else.

When we step into Christianity, we're told to "live like Jesus" and "be like Jesus." We wear our WWJD bracelets and spend our lives trying to imitate what we see Jesus doing in the Bible. But that's impossible. And that's not the goal.

God isn't trying to get us to be like somebody else. Nor is He telling us to try our best to imitate Him. Instead, He wants us to see that we're already like Jesus. Right now, we're like Him. This doesn't mean we *are* Jesus. But the same acceptance, holiness, and worth that Jesus has, we have. The good news

"
The same acceptance, holiness, and worth that Jesus has, we have.
"

of Christianity is that God treats us like Jesus! We're as loved, accepted, and favored as Jesus Himself. How? Jesus took what we deserved so that we could get what He deserved.

Jesus is the perfect image of God, and in Christ we have been recreated in that image. We're little statues of God all over this world. That's right. When people see you, they see a glimpse of God. You're his reflection. How? Christ is in you!

The beauty of Christianity is that God uses our personalities to display His love to the world. Yes, we're called to love like Jesus, but we do this only by receiving His love and letting Him love through us. It's like dancing. We aren't watching Jesus dance and then trying to copy Him. Instead, He's our partner and we're following His lead as He guides us through the dance of life. Even this analogy doesn't fully capture it, because Christ is living on the inside of us.

Here's the great thing: the Bible says that our destiny is to reflect Jesus in how we live. We can't get away from it, because God is going to make it happen. So we don't have to try to make it happen. Instead, we just trust Jesus.

You see, all religions follow some historical teacher and then instruct everyone to try their best to be like him. But Christianity is different. Our Teacher lives in us and is living His life through each one of us. Sure, our lives will look like His. We'll love people

Our Teacher lives in us and is living His life through each one of us.

radically; we'll serve and give. But we don't have to wake up each day and try to be something we're not. Instead, we just get to be who God has made us, knowing we're already like Him.

When I finally got to high school, I was still trying to be like Jordan Shipley. I was so excited to play for Burnet High School in front of thousands of people every Friday night, and prove to people how good I was. More than anything, I just wanted to be like my hero.

I'll never forget it. After I'd had a good game and scored a few touchdowns, a seven-year-old boy came up to me after the game, wearing my number. "Zach," he said, "when I grow up, I want to be just like you."

It hit me. This whole time I was trying to be somebody else, not realizing that who I am is already enough. I was impressive. I was good. I'd failed to see that I was unique and that no one else was like me.

I no longer felt the need to try to be Jordan, or anyone else for that matter. Instead, I became confident in who I was and simply lived from that. Affirmation does that. That's what the Holy Spirit in you is doing. He isn't trying to get rid of you; instead, He's affirming who God has made you.

Hearing God's Opinion

"You're already everything I want you to be. There's nothing to fix. And there's nothing for you to hide. Embrace yourself and see how special you are to Me. You don't need to get out of the way, and I don't want to get rid of you. You and I are a dream team. I've uniquely created you to express Me like no one else can. Stop striving to be like Me. You're My kid, and you've got My DNA. Just be all that I've made you to be."

20

Lacking Nothing

And my God will meet all your needs
according to the riches of his glory in Christ Jesus.
Philippians 4:19 NIV

Do you sometimes feel like God has forgotten about you? Or that He isn't concerned about what you're going through? Me too. And the people who were with Jesus for three years sometimes felt the same way.

One of my favorite stories about Jesus is when He was taking a nap in a boat in the middle of a storm. He was with His disciples as they were crossing a sea to get to the other side. All of a sudden, a storm came from nowhere and created waves that started filling the boat.

Now, most of Jesus's disciples were professional fishermen. They knew how to handle the water and weren't scared of storms. But this storm was different. They were freaking out. It must have been like hurricane weather. They all thought they were going to die.

They woke Jesus up from His nap and said, "Don't You care that we're dying?" Then Jesus calmed the storm, and He asked them, "Why are you scared? Have you no trust in Me?"

Notice that Jesus didn't create that storm. And He isn't the creator of your bad circumstances. But He does calm the storm. And He's the author of our faith and our peace in every storm.

What I love about this story is that Jesus doesn't calm the storm because the disciples had a lot of faith. Actually, they had no faith. Yet Jesus met their need. That's the good news of Christianity: Jesus is faithful even when we're faithless. Jesus is with us even in the midst of our loneliness and worst moments.

> *Jesus is with us even in the midst of our loneliness and worst moments.*

Jesus knows our needs and cares about us deeply. He promises to never leave us. He never forces us to figure things out on our own. He assures us that He'll give us everything we need.

Are you looking for value, significance, acceptance, love, and peace? Look to Jesus, and recognize that in Him you're valued, you're significant, you're loved, and you're accepted. He is your peace, and you're worth everything to Him.

The Bible says that Jesus is our Shepherd, and in Him we lack nothing. It says that He leads us, refreshes us, guides us, is always with us, and is always good and loving toward us.

***

I remember a time in ministry when I'd lost all hope. I was burned out and sad, and felt like no one cared about me. After a Wednesday night youth service, I was driving home and felt like giving up on everything. I thought, *If I disappear, will anyone notice or care?* It was perhaps the lowest point of my life. Life didn't seem worth living.

I finally started talking to God. It was more yelling than anything, but I talked to Him as I was driving and expressed my concerns and needs and frustrations. What was weird is that I'd spent the previous months hiding from God and from others. I was real good at faking like everything was okay.

But once I opened up to God that night, everything changed. I shared with Him what I wanted and needed. I didn't feel like He was enough, and I felt like I was lacking. I needed validation, significance, and worth.

That was one of the most freeing experiences in my life. I'd stopped talking to God about my concerns and needs. I knew that He was enough, but I was trying to hide my neediness. I was trying to fake it with God. Funny, I know.

He didn't answer me that night with an audible voice. God doesn't talk to me that way. But over the next week, He opened my eyes to the people around me who were loving and affirming me. And He opened my eyes to the riches of His life in me. He taught me that He is I Am: "I am everything you need Me to be. I am enough for you."

He showed me that in my weakness He is strong. He showed me that the goal isn't to be strong or to act like I have it all together; instead, the goal is to trust Him. I realized that being me—no matter what that looks like on a given day—is more freeing than being a fake version of somebody else.

> " I realized that being me—no matter what that looks like on a given day—is more freeing than being a fake version of somebody else. "

There's a story in the Old Testament about God giving bread to His people. But the catch was, they couldn't store it or save it for the next day. Instead, they would have to trust that He would provide new bread each day. And He did. The same is true for us. God wants to meet our needs in each moment. We can't expect to live off the way He met a need yesterday; instead, He's inviting us to trust Him every moment of every day to meet every new need.

And in Him, we have all we need. We're one choice away from trusting Him to get our needs met. The other option is to try to get our needs met through other people, things, or activities. But those resources won't last. So talk to God, be reai with what you need, and lean into Him as your source for everything.

Since Christ is in you, you lack nothing. You have everything you need. He is the bread of life, and He promises that in Him we will never hunger or thirst.

Hearing God's Opinion

"No matter what valley you go through, I'll be there with you. I'm your peace in the midst of it all. I'll comfort, strengthen, and establish you in My grace. Don't be afraid. I'm your help in the midst of trouble. I promise to protect you. You'll face trouble, but trust in Me. I've overcome the world."

21

Secure

I give them eternal life, and they shall never perish;
no one will snatch them out of my hand.

John 10:28 NIV

I almost died. Well, sort of.

I was about ten years old, and my brother took me to a place called Devil's Waterhole. Scary, right? This place had a huge cliff where you could jump off into the water. All my brother's friends were doing this, making it look easy.

If you don't know me, I'm short. There's a reason God made me this way; I'm afraid of heights. If I was tall, I'd be walking around scared all the time. Think about it. Looking down at my shoes would terrify me.

Anyway, I wanted to impress my brother and his friends. After they trash-talked me for a while, I mustered up the courage to climb up onto that cliff. It felt like I was on a cloud, but not cloud nine. I was scared to death.

Finally, after accepting Jesus into my heart, I prayed my last prayer and jumped.

What a thrill! It was one of the most exciting things I've ever done!

Fear does that to us. Fear lies to us, telling us things that aren't true and exaggerating everything. Fear says that God won't love us, that God is mad at us. Fear says that we're a mistake. Fear says that God will leave us, that we'll lose God if we sin too much.

Fear is a liar.

But God has set us free from fear. God has deep affection for us. And God promises us security and freedom. If what you're hearing isn't liberating you, then it's not from God.

If what you're hearing isn't liberating you, then it's not from God.

Sometimes it can be scary to trust God. Just like I was terrified to jump off that rock. Sometimes it's easier to listen to fear. But I promise you, you'll never regret trusting Jesus. Take those thoughts and compare them to God's Word. Then choose to dwell on and trust in God's opinion, not in your fears.

Don't be afraid. That's something Jesus tells us again and again throughout the Bible. Right before Peter walked on water, Jesus told the disciples, "Don't be afraid." We don't have to be afraid, because He is within us. We don't have to fear, because we're secure in Jesus. He's got us. He's with us. And He has our best in mind.

> "We don't have to fear, because we're secure in Jesus. He's got us. He's with us. And He has our best in mind."

The lie is that we think, with enough sin, we can undo what God has done. But the Bible says His grace is abundant. Our God is bigger than our mistakes. We cannot undo what He has finished. And His mercy and kindness are greater than our failures.

***

There's a well-known story about a group of blind men who were walking along and unknowingly encountered an elephant in the road. They tried to identify this obstacle by what they could feel. One felt the trunk and thought it was a snake. One felt the tusk and thought it was a pipe. One felt the leg and thought it was a tree trunk. Another felt the tail and thought it was rope.

The men argued about which of them was right, until finally the person riding the elephant let them know what it was. The men all realized they were drawing conclusions from only partial information.

Many of us grab on to one thing we do or have done, and make it our entire identity. So often we have an incomplete view of who we are. We most often define ourselves by one thing, something that's external. But everything external changes. We won't be an athlete forever. We won't always be young. We won't always be successful. We won't always have the same profession.

Here's good news: Our identity in Christ never changes. It's unshakeable. It's something we cannot get away from. Once we're a child of God, we cannot lose that. We're locked in for good.

Safe, secure, hidden, sealed, and untouchable—this is how the Bible describes our relationship with God. We're safe in His hands, and nothing can take us away. We're secure in His grace; nothing can separate us. We're sealed by His Spirit; nothing can remove us from His presence. And we cannot be touched by the evil one.

Hearing God's Opinion

"I'll always be faithful to you, even when you're faithless. Nothing can separate you from Me. Nothing can take you away from the security of My hand. It's not about your hold on Me, but My hold on you. You're secure in Me. You're seated with Me in heaven, and the life I give you is eternal."

Righteous

God made him who had no sin to be sin for us,

so that in him we might become the righteousness of God.

2 Corinthians 5:21 NIV

Have you ever been pulled over? Me too. I'd just finished one of my best high school football games. I mean, I played amazing. As I made my way home, basking in my accomplishments, I heard and saw behind me those Christmas lights. You know, the ones that blind you, not cheer you up.

I grew up in a small town where everybody knew everybody, so I thought for sure this guy would know me. I mean after all, I did just have an amazing game.

He walked up to my truck and said, "You were speeding. License and registration please."

I reached into my pockets. Nothing. I turned them inside out, thinking my wallet was hiding, but nothing. I'd left my wallet in my locker. I looked at the officer with my best impersonation of a small cat begging for food. I think I looked like a crazy person. So like a crazy person—I mean cat—I shrugged my shoulders and said, "I've got no ID."

That didn't seem to work, so I told the officer, "I'm Zach Maldonado, and I just had this awesome game. I'm the captain of the football team. And I make good grades. And look." I grabbed a newspaper lying on the seat and showed him my front-page appearance a few weeks before. "This is me!"

Look, I know what you're thinking. *What kind of guy does this?* But I didn't know my identity back then. Give me a break. Trying to prove our identity can be tough. And for many of us, this is what life's about: proving ourselves to someone else.

In the Bible, we see religious people trying to prove their identity to God, but this will never measure up. It's never good enough, because God wants our trust more than our performance.

Even after hearing and knowing our identity, when shame and guilt comes, we still can struggle to remember who we are. We're asked about our identity, and immediately we answer with a list of our accomplishments, our status, or what we've done for God. This question confronts us like the police officer. And if we're honest, we're left shrugging our shoulders and trying to prove ourselves.

It's easy for us to jump back on the treadmill of performing for our identity. But the work isn't to do something in order to get our identity. Jesus said the work is to believe our identity is true.

> "
> *The work isn't to do something in order to get our identity. Jesus said the work is to believe our identity is true.*
> "

Jesus became our sin—every single one of our sins. Why? So that you and I could become children of God who are right and good with God. The Bible says we're the righteousness of God. We're as right with God as Jesus is.

Unlike the religious people, our answer to that question

is no longer based on what we do, but on what Jesus has done. I'm the righteousness of God because of Jesus, not because of what I do.

Jesus gave us a great analogy when He said that whoever hears His words and acts on them is like a wise person who built his house on a rock. Such a person is wise, Jesus said, because when storms and rain came, their house will always stand. Jesus also said that whoever hears His words and does *not* act on them is like someone who builds his house on sand; that guy's foolish, because his house will be washed away by the first storm that comes along.

When our worth, righteousness, and value come from Jesus alone, we're building our identity on the Rock, which is Jesus Christ. This is crucial. Accomplishments, status, wealth, popularity—all that is sand. They won't hold up.

Nothing can change who we are in Christ. Nothing.

Think about everything you've been called, every label the world has given you. Everything—every mistake and label—Jesus took on the cross for you. Now think about everything we call God—holy, righteous, perfect, clean, good.

He gave that to you. For free. No catch. No strings attached.

This doesn't mean we always live good or think right. That's the process we're still in. But our core identity is fixed. It won't change. We're already all that God wants us to be. Now He's conforming us to

" *We're already all that God wants us to be.* "

Himself and teaching us to live out what's already true of us.

The father of one of my friends was a police officer and happened to be driving by while I was pulled over. He recognized my vehicle and advocated on my behalf by telling the officer who I was and that he knew me well. Because of my relationship with my friend's dad, I didn't get a ticket that night.

My friend's dad is a picture of Jesus to us. When we get accused and forget our identity, God is always showing us and reminding us of who we are in Him. And more importantly, *Whose* we are. We are God's righteous children. He never leaves us empty-handed. He never asks us to prove ourselves. And since we have relationship with Him, He is always supporting and defending us.

Hearing God's Opinion

"I became all the sin you'll ever commit so that you could become all the righteousness that is Mine. You are now good at your core. You're not a bad person trying to be good. No, you're righteous, holy, blameless, and new. You were never meant to carry shame and guilt. I took all that at the cross. Leave it behind; it can no longer define you or have power over you. The truest thing about you is that you're righteous, no matter what you do, will do, or have done."

23

Obedient

But thanks be to God that though you were slaves of sin,
you became obedient from the heart to that form of teaching
to which you were committed.

Romans 6:17

There were two sisters in the Bible named Martha and Mary. One day Jesus stopped in at their house. The women decided to do two different things. Martha chose to do things for Jesus, while Mary chose to sit at His feet.

If I'm honest, I'm Martha in this story. I mean, I would be cleaning my house and trying to figure out what to cook and serve Jesus. I'm a people pleaser. I'd probably just order Domino's, but that's beside the point. I think we can relate to Martha because we live in a nonstop world. We're always going.

Anyway, Martha was distracted, and she asked Jesus, "Do you not care?" I've asked this to God more times than I can count. Maybe you've done the same.

Jesus answers her by saying, "You are worried and anxious about a lot of things, but only one thing matters, and your sister has discovered it." What did Mary discover? Resting at Jesus's feet is what matters. Jesus wants our attention more than He wants our activity.

> "Jesus wants our attention more than He wants our activity."

Here's what I love about this story: if Jesus needed something, who would have been able to get it for Him? Mary, because she was at His feet, available to Him. Notice that Jesus doesn't say serving is bad. Instead, He wants us to examine where our focus is.

We're not called to do things for God because we have to, or because we feel some responsibility. Nor do we do things for God to get a need met. He promises to meet our needs, and He doesn't need us.

Instead, God is inviting us to participate with Him in His work. We do things for God as a child, not as a slave. He's our Father, not our employer. So God is calling us to this new way. It's not about striving but about trusting. We don't do things in order to get God's attention, as Martha did. Instead, like Mary, we do things with Jesus. Put another way, we depend on and trust Jesus's life in us to motivate and inspire us.

Our obedience to God follows our identity. Our obedience is the fruit, not the cause, of our identity. We obey because we're loved, accepted, forgiven, and secure in Christ. We don't obey to make God happy or to get Him to love us.

> "
> *We obey because we're loved, accepted, forgiven, and secure in Christ.*
> "

Jesus gave us a new command: to love others from the love He has given us. We have to first be loved before we can love. We have to sit at Jesus's feet and receive His love and rest before we can go out and love other people. It's from Jesus's love that we live, not for it.

Jesus invites us to rest in Him, and then He calls us to live from that rest. Obedience, serving, giving, and loving others take on a whole new meaning when we realize we do those things because we want to, not because we have to. We do them because God is in love with us, not in order to get God to love us.

The Bible goes even deeper than that. It says that we've become obedient and loving from the core of our being. From our heart we want to give and serve and love others. So are you looking to find fulfillment? It won't come from doing nothing. Christ in you is active and longs to express Himself through you. That's why the good works He has for you have already been planned out. Our job is just be available to God and to walk in those good works He's already planned.

The good news about your new identity in Jesus is that you no longer want to sin. You want what God wants. Sure, sometimes it feels like you want to sin. And maybe

"
The good news about your new identity in Jesus is that you no longer want to sin.
"

you're struggling with sin right now. But the truth is, you'll find satisfaction only when you trust Jesus.

Christ in you gives you the power to love others. As an accepted person and someone filled with Christ, you can accept people. As someone filled with God's love, you can love others. As someone who has been forgiven totally, you can forgive without condition. As someone who has been treated with unconditional kindness, you can treat others with over-the-top love. Your nature is now like this. At the core of your being, you're a loving person.

The work is finished. We're not trying to gain any more acceptance, security, forgiveness, or peace with God. We live under God's declaration of, "It is finished," not "Do more," or "Be more."

> We live under God's declaration of, "It is finished," not "Do more," or "Be more."

Since Christ is in us, everything we encounter in life provides the context in which we experience Jesus in new ways. At my job, I get to experience Christ as my strength and endurance as He gets me through each day. With difficult family members, I get to experience Christ as my patience and love. In my relationships, I get to experience God's love for me and God's work through me. Through each circumstance and relationship, I get to know Christ more. That's the goal of our life. It's not about doing more or being better; it's about knowing Him. And knowing Him changes everything.

Hearing God's Opinion

"I've made you obedient. I know that word can be scary, but remember, your obedience never earns anything. If you never obey another day in your life, I'll always love you and accept you. This means you don't have to freak out over whether you're obeying enough. It's not about that. You're already enough before you ever obey. I've made it so that obedience feels natural, just like breathing. As you trust Me, obedience will naturally follow. Loving others is your new desire."

24

Child of God

But to all who did receive him, who believed in his name,

he gave the right to become children of God.

John 1:12 ESV

I was your typical class clown. My elementary school teachers either loved me or hated me; there was no in between. As class clown, my job was to always make other students laugh, even at my own expense. Most days, I would find a way to outsmart my teachers to get a laugh out of my classmates or to just make myself feel better.

One day, though, that changed. My science teacher was discussing gravity with us. Trying to outsmart this teacher, I said, "I can't see, taste, touch, smell, or hear gravity.

Therefore it's not real!" I got an *ooh* from my classmates, the kind you get when you've really dissed the teacher—like when rappers are battling and they make a good rap. Or something like that.

Anyway, I was thinking I surely outsmarted my teacher, but he quickly said, "Zach, by that logic, you can't see, taste, touch, smell, or hear your brain. Therefore you're brainless!"

I still haven't quite recovered from that burn. But there are truths about God and our identity that aren't based on what we experience or what our senses tell us. They're true no matter what we think, see, hear, touch, or taste.

Some days we'll feel weird and bad, and no amount of rehearsing our identity will make us feel better. That's life. Jesus didn't promise us perfect emotions or thoughts. But there's a knowledge we can have despite the feelings we experience. That's what faith is. If we can believe God created us and raised Jesus from the dead, then we can believe in His opinion of us even in the midst of accusations and emotional turmoil.

We're God's children no matter what. This means He'll never leave us. We're always in the family. There's nothing you or I can do to lose this. At times we may feel alone, forsaken, or lost, but God promises that He'll never leave us.

" We're God's children no matter what. This means He'll never leave us. We're always in the family. There's nothing you or I can do to lose this. "

To be a child of God means to be at peace with God. Do you realize that God isn't mad at you? You and God are good. He's not angry or frustrated with you. You're His child, which means He treats you just like He treats Jesus.

To be a child of God means to be an heir. Everything that God has is yours. By his goodness and love, He has given us everything He has to offer. He's holding back nothing. We don't work for or earn an inheritance; instead, it's given to us because we're in the family.

To be a child of God means being God's friend. More like His best friend. He absolutely loves hanging out inside you. It's His favorite thing to do. We're not God's enemies. Nor are we somehow in God's way. We're His friends, which means everything that God wants to do in this world, He wants to include us in. He's never going to leave us out. He wants you involved because He and you are compatible. God and you united together make a great team. Jesus looks good in you.

" God and you united together make a great team. Jesus looks good in you. "

And your expression of Him is quite the sight to see.

To be a child of God means we're standing in God's kindness and power, rooted in His love, hidden in His Son, and guarded by His peace and presence. You and I won't always feel loved, accepted, forgiven, or indwelt by God. But it's not about feeling the presence of God's love, acceptance, or Spirit; it's about knowing, no matter what we feel in a given moment, that God is fully with us, completely in love with us, and has never-ending acceptance of us.

To be a child of God means that nothing is wrong with you. Complete, pleasing, accepted, loved, qualified, wonderfully made, united, a masterpiece, flawless, blessed, saved, forgiven, like Jesus, secure, righteous, and obedient—that's real, and that's who you are.

Hearing God's Opinion

"I promise to spend the rest of eternity reminding you of this: There's nothing wrong with you, My child. I know this sounds too good to be true, but My opinion of you is real. It's how it is. Remember, it's not about doing right or doing wrong; it's about trusting Me in every moment. You're not what you do. You're not what you've done. You're all that I say you are. You're My beloved child—amazing, special, perfectly made, and fully pleasing to Me. I love you so much!"

25

Now What?

Therefore, as you have received Christ Jesus the Lord,

so walk in Him.

Colossians 2:6

Now it's time to live. You get to be all that God has made you to be. This means you get to be yourself. You're going to spend the rest of your life learning and relearning the truth about who you are in Christ. We don't graduate from our need of God's grace; instead, we simply grow in our dependence upon His scandalous grace. You received Christ by trusting Him, so walk and live by trusting in who He says He is and who He says you are.

This will feel normal. God doesn't promise perfect

emotions. And Christ living His life through you feels like you being who He's made you. It feels like you're being yourself. So don't over analyze, just live.

There will be days when it feels like your new identity isn't real. And many people may try to say it isn't true.

That's why I created the "Who I Am in Christ" section, with over seventy Bible verses all about our new identity in Christ. Sink your teeth into those. Go to God's Word and read them and see for yourself God's opinion of you.

Our minds are being renewed and our behavior is slowly lining up with who God has already made us. And that's okay. That's the process we are all in. That's why we need community. We need other people to live this life with. To hash out what it means to be a new creation. To share our struggles and to bear one another's burdens.

Share this book with friends. Gather with them, read it with them, or use the book as a coaster and talk about what your new identity means to you. Everyone needs to know who they are in Christ.

If you have a question, need help finding a

community in your area, or just want to talk, you can email

me – zacmaldo@gmail.com

Who I Am in Chris

- » I'm complete in Christ. (Colossians 2:10)

- » I'm a pleasing aroma to God. (2 Corinthians 2:15)

- » I'm accepted and approved by God. (Romans 15:7)

- » I'm deeply and dearly loved. (John 3:16; Romans 8:38–39)

- » I'm delighted in by God. (Zephaniah 3:17)

- » I'm fully qualified to minster and be used by God. (2 Corinthians 3:6)

- » I'm wonderfully made. (Psalm 139:14)

- » I'm blameless. (Colossians 1:22; Jude 24)

- » I'm united to Christ—one spirit with Him. (Romans 6:5; 1 Corinthians 6:17)

- » I'm God's masterpiece. (Ephesians 2:10)

- » I'm flawless and perfect. (Hebrews 10:14)

- » I'm blessed with every spiritual blessing. (Ephesians 1:3)

- » I'm completely saved forever. (Ephesians 2:8–9; Hebrews 7:25; 1 Peter 1:3–5)

- » I'll never be punished. (Romans 8:1)

- » I've been set free from sin's power. (Romans 6:14)

» I'm forgiven of all my sins—past, present, and future. (Colossians 2:13; 1 John 2:12; Hebrews 10:18)

» I'm just like Jesus. (1 John 4:17)

» I lack nothing. (Philippians 4:19; Psalm 23)

» I'm safe and secure in Christ. (John 10:28)

» I'm the righteousness of God. (2 Corinthians 5:21)

» I'm obedient. (Romans 6:17)

» I'm God's child. (John 1:12)

» I'm close to God. (Ephesians 2:13)

» I'm never alone. (Hebrews 13:5)

» I'm new. (2 Corinthians 5:17)

» I'm at peace with God. (Romans 5:1)

» I'm seated with Christ in the heavenlies. (Ephesians 2:6)

» I'm chosen, set apart, and dearly loved. (Colossians 3:12)

» I'm a child of light. (1 Thessalonians 5:5)

» I'm a partaker of the divine nature. (2 Peter 1:4)

» I'm part of a chosen race, a royal priesthood, a set-apart nation; I'm God's own possession. (1 Peter 2:9–10)

» I'm anointed. (1 John 2:27)

» I'm born of God. (1 John 5:8)

- » I'm holy. (Hebrews 10:10)

- » I'm a slave to righteousness. (Romans 6:18)

- » I'm right with God. (Romans 3:24; 5:1)

- » I'm more than a conqueror. (Romans 8:37)

- » I'm in Christ. (1 Corinthians 1:30)

- » I'm sealed by the Holy Spirit. (Ephesians 1:13; 4:30)

- » I'm redeemed. (Colossians 1:14; Ephesians 1:7)

- » I'm alive. (Ephesians 2:5)

- » I'm dead to sin. (Romans 6:11)

- » I'm a saint. (Ephesians 1:1; Colossians 1:2)

- » I'm a friend of God. (John 15:15)

- » I'm God's temple. (1 Corinthians 6:19)

- » I'm God's beloved child. (Ephesians 5:1)

- » I'm a citizen of heaven. (Philippians 3:20; Luke 10:20)

- » I'm free from the law. (Galatians 5:18)

- » I'm hidden with Christ in God. (Colossians 3:3)

- » I'm faithful. (Ephesians 1:1)

- » I'm washed, sanctified, and justified. (1 Corinthians 6:11)

- » I'm cared for by God. (1 Peter 5:7)

- » I have the mind of Christ. (1 Corinthians 2:16)

» I have everything I need for life and godliness. (2 Peter 1:3)

» I've been crucified, buried, and raised to new life in Christ. (Galatians 2:20; Romans 6:4-6)

» God has forgotten my sins. (Hebrews 8:12)

» God's not mad at me. (Isaiah 54:9)

» God's not ashamed of me. (Hebrews 2:11; Hebrews 11:16)

Acknowledgments

I want to first thank my beautiful fiancé, Grace. I dedicated this book to you because you have taught me so much about my identity in Christ and you have been God's instrument for so much healing and freedom for me. Thank you for all your love and support during the process of writing and completing this book. I love you so much!

I want to thank my family and friends for all their love, prayers, and encouragement. I am so thankful to have each of you on my side! In addition, I want to thank my friend and co-laborer in Christ, Andrew Farley. Thank you for always being there for me, for encouraging me, teaching me, and pointing me to Christ!

Thank you, John Lynch, for helping me with the title, for your encouragement during this process, and for being a voice of truth in my life.

Also, I want to acknowledge everyone at Church Without Religion! Thank you for being such an encouraging and loving body to me. And thank you for supporting this book and making it a reality!

Zach Maldonado serves as a pastor at Church Without Religion and with Andrew Farley Ministries. Zach is the author of *The Cross Worked.* and a speaker with a passion to proclaim the gospel. He holds a Master of Arts in Theology degree from Fuller Theological Seminary. Connect personally with Zach on Instagram, Twitter, and Facebook (@ZachMaldo).

THE**CROSS** WORKED.

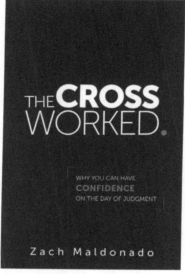

Do you doubt God's goodness? Are you fearful that He will judge you for your mistakes?

In The Cross Worked., Zach Maldonado explores the Scriptures about forgiveness, reward, and judgment, and dismantles the popular religious jargon around these verses, helping readers:

- Discover the forgiveness they have in Christ.
- Overcome their fear of God's judgment.
- Know the goodness and love of God.

By the end of The Cross Worked. you'll understand how to enjoy Jesus and live each day with confidence!

AVAILABLE NOW ON AMAZON!

CPSIA information can be obtained
at www.ICGtesting.com
Printed in the USA
FSHW021237200919
62164FS

9 780578 527611